RACIAL INEQUALITY IN MATHEMATICS EDUCATION

STUDIES IN EDUCATIONAL ETHNOGRAPHY

Series Editor: Professor Rodney Hopson, University of Illinois-Urbana Champaign, USA

Studies in Educational Ethnography presents original research monographs and edited volumes based on ethnographic perspectives, theories, and methodologies. Such research will advance the development of theory, practice, policy, and praxis for improving schooling and education in neighborhood, community, and global contexts.

In complex neighborhood, community, and global contexts, educational ethnographies should situate themselves beyond isolated classrooms or single sites and concern themselves with more than narrow methodological pursuits. Rather, the ethnographic research, perspectives and methodologies featured in this series extend our understandings of sociocultural educational phenomena and their global and local meanings.

Forthcoming in the Series

Neoliberalism and Inclusive Education
Sylvia Mac

Black Boys' Lived and Everyday Experiences in STEM
KiMi Wilson

Ethnography of Monitoring and Evaluation Efforts; Large-scale Data and Citizen Engagement in India's Education System
Melissa Rae Goodnight

Ethics, Ethnography and Education
Edited by Lisa Russell, Jonathan Tummons, and Ruth Barley

RACIAL INEQUALITY IN MATHEMATICS EDUCATION

Exploring Academic Identity as a Sense of Belonging

BY

THIERRY ELIN-SAINTINE
Stockton University, USA

United Kingdom – North America – Japan – India
Malaysia – China

Emerald Publishing Limited
Howard House, Wagon Lane, Bingley BD16 1WA, UK

First edition 2021

Reprints and permissions service
Contact: permissions@emeraldinsight.com

British Library Cataloguing in Publication Data
A catalogue record for this book is available from the British Library

ISBN: 978-1-78769-886-4 (Print)
ISBN: 978-1-80043-990-0 (Online)
ISBN: 978-1-80043-992-4 (Epub)

ISOQAR certified
Management System,
awarded to Emerald
for adherence to
Environmental
standard
ISO 14001:2004.

Certificate Number 1985
ISO 14001

INVESTOR IN PEOPLE

This project is dedicated to my wife Rachel and my son Gabriel. This journey would never have made it past a dream, and bar stools banter without their unconditional love, support, patience, and Rachel's unyielding commitment to a more equitable tomorrow. I would be remiss if I did not take this opportunity to also thank Rachel for the countless feedback and always constructive criticism. Thank You. I love you.

Praise for *Racial Inequality in Mathematics Education*

"This book skillfully unpacks the complexities of race, academic identity, and learning in a Philadelphia high school classroom. Saintine asks: what does it mean to be a "math person" and why is this problematic myth so durable? As a mathematics professor with an impressive background in performing arts, creative writing, and urban education, Saintine rejects the dualistic and overly simplistic idea that the world can be parsed into math persons and nonmath people. This is a wonderful ethnography that elevates Black and Latinx students' voices and reflections on themselves and their school. The book calls for a new social imaginary that begins with a reconceptualization of math education in urban schools."

Will J. Jordan, Temple University, USA

"This text is a must-read for preservice and in-service teachers of mathematics to examine the ways in which mathematics education continues to limit opportunities for Black students. Myths about who is and who is not a math person are pervasive and continue to dissuade historically excluded students from persisting in mathematics as a discipline. Flin-Saintine presents the results of an ethnographic study that examines academic identity and sense of belonging among a group of Black high schools students in an honor's precalculus class. The counterstories that emerge from this study challenge age-old assumptions and help teachers to understand the complex nature of mathematics learning in a race-based society. Most importantly, the text offers teaching strategies to foster the development of academic identity in Black students who, as a racial/ethnic group, have the brilliance to succeed in advanced mathematics courses."

Jacqueline Leonard, PhD, University of Wyoming, USA

"This book is a very welcome addition to recent scholarship on race, identity, and mathematics education. Pushing back on stereotypes and commonsense ideas about who can do mathematics, this book makes explicit how concepts like ability and competence are not innate traits of a select few but are contested and negotiated opportunities that are readily made available to some students and denied to others. This book – through the voices and experiences of young people – ask readers to think about who gets to be considered a legitimate doer of mathematics, under what circumstances, and with what material consequences. This intellectually honest case study will challenge teachers to rethink their roles in these negotiations. More broadly, this book will appeal to mathematics education researchers, graduate students, in-service and preservice teachers, school administrators, policy makers, and others who are interested in the realities of race in schools but who are also willing to engage in antiracist practice. For all who pick up this book, I urge three things: listen, hear, and act."

Danny Bernard Martin, University of Illinois at Chicago

"Professor Elin-Saintine's work demonstrates clearly how identity is central to the learning process. Further, he shows that ideas about race are not just attitudes that individuals have about other individuals, but that racism is built into the structure of our educational institutions and the culture of math education. And those attitudes flourish because they are disguised behind ideas of what it means to be good at math. As such, this work stands to advance our understanding of how to support students of mathematics from diverse backgrounds. Further, it will be a support for practitioners in the field seeking to better understand how to mentor their students."

Wesley Shumar, Professor, Department of Communication, Affiliated Faculty, School of Education, Drexel University

CONTENTS

SERIES EDITOR PREFACE

Thierry Saintine's book, *Racial inequality in mathematics education: Exploring academic identity as a sense of belonging*, is a second book to be published in the *Studies in Educational Ethnography* book series most recently focused on African American boys and their academic achievement in the science, technology, engineering, and mathematics (STEM) context of schooling and education in the United States. Saintine tackles age-old race-based narratives and myths about ability and ideologies about success in mathematics among Black students, while interrogating beliefs and notions about a racial pyramid of academic ability in general. His ethnographic study provides counterstories and narratives of academic identity and sense of belonging among a group of Black students that society most easily casts off and forgotten, despite their brilliance.

Saintine's work extends the new directions in educational ethnography in the 21st century and the purpose of this reconstituted book series and international and student advisory board development over the last 5 years to study classrooms and educational communities with a concomitant reading of broader structural forces, giving meaning to these complex neighborhood, community, and global contexts. His book contributes to larger conversations about the forces and systems that contribute to mathematics, STEM broadly, and inequities in American education.

The birth of the series in the mid-2000s by Prof. Geoffrey Walford (Oxford University) spearheaded ethnographic research, perspectives and methodologies featured that would extend our understandings of sociocultural educational phenomena and their global and local meanings. One important community of scholars of ethnography was through Ethnography and Education conferences initially held at St. Hilda's College. *Racial inequality in mathematics education: Exploring academic identity as a sense of belonging* is the third book in the new volume home within the College of Education, University of Illinois-Urbana Champaign. Located in the Quantitative and Qualitative Methodology, Measurement, and Evaluation (QUERIES), Department of Educational Psychology, the College of Education has been the academic home to multiple traditions of research and evaluation scholarship in humanities and social sciences for decades and the International Congress of Qualitative Inquiry (ICQI) which hosts hundreds of scholars and practitioners who travel from around the world to the cornfields of Illinois.

Just as Walford utilized UK and European networks to expand the reach of the series, the volume home takes advantage of the special interest groups, divisions, and associations such as the Ethnography of Education Forum at the University of Pennsylvania, Council on Anthropology and Education/American Anthropological Association and the American Educational Research Association (AERA) and other associations in the US and North America.

Further details about the book series are available through the Emerald website or from the Series Editor.

Rodney Hopson
Series Editor

ABOUT THE AUTHOR

Thierry Elin-Saintine is an Assistant Professor of Mathematics at Stockton University, USA. He holds a PhD in Urban Education, concentration in mathematics education, from Temple University. Elin-Saintine's research interests revolve around the idea of academic learning as a social practice; he focuses on academic identity defined as a sense of belonging.

FOREWORD

This book is based on data collected for my dissertation during the 2015–16 academic year. At the time, a book seemed like a fantasy, a very distant and nearly unimaginable possibility. Receiving the 2017–18 Concha Delgado Gaitán's Presidential Fellowship, and joining the Council on Anthropology and Education (CAE) community provided me the confidence, support – special thanks to Dr. Rodney Hopson – space, and clarity necessary to begin this project. The CAE community helped me realize that the stories of 11 Black and Brown teenagers from northeast Philadelphia seeking to make sense of their classrooms' experiences in relationship to the mythical "math person" are part of the fight for more "anti-oppressive" educational experiences.

My path to the field of mathematics education is a bit unusual and unorthodox. I hold a PhD in Urban Education from Temple University, and a Master's of Arts in mathematics education and a Master's of Fine Arts in creative writing and literature from the City College of New York. Prior to my many years in graduate school, I was actively pursuing a career in theatre arts and film. My disparate professional experiences and mismatched credentials are not here to suggest or imply something "special" or "unique" about me. They're here to explain *belonging*. Being an immigrant, Black, with an incongruous set of academic and work experiences developed in predominantly white institutions (PWIs), belonging has always been central and foundational to my self-concept and emerging identity as a researcher.

Belonging is now one of the guiding principles of how I think about and study inequity in education. Framing and exploring academic identity as belonging in this book was not much of a leap. It was out of necessity, a need to understand and toil with some of the muted truths about the American education experiment.

ACKNOWLEDGMENTS

I need to acknowledge another very special person in my life, my mother, Marie B. Bonhomette. Words can only betray the depth of my gratitude for the sacrifices, the love, and boundless caring. Still, I thank you for the human you have allowed and challenged me to become.

I also want to acknowledge others who have knowingly or unwittingly helped me on this journey. I extend my deepest gratitude to the faculty members of the Brooklyn College's Africana Studies and Political Studies Departments – a special thank you to Dr. George Cunnhingham – who introduced me to the world of academia. To the City College of New York's Graduate English and Mathematics departments, thank you for fueling the fire under my love for words, the performing arts, teaching, and mathematics.

Finally, I want to thank the Temple University's Urban Education and Teaching and Learning Departments. Special thanks to Dr. Will J. Jordan who has been integral to my academic development and emerging identity as a researcher. I am grateful for Drs. Maia Cucchiara, Carol Brandt, and Kristie Newton for the research assistantship opportunities that have undoubtedly provided me the skills and confidence needed to complete this project.

This would not be possible without the students and teaching staff who agreed to be part of this study. Thank you for your time and for making me a part of your community.

INTRODUCTION

It is commonplace to hear stories of success or struggle in mathematics linked to genes. For many, a penchant for the arts is justification for negative experiences in mathematics. Others, often proudly, correlate careers in science, technology, engineering, and mathematics (STEM) fields with presumed creative deficiencies. One of the reasons is the widely accepted notion that people are born with either "math genes" or a natural aptitude for the arts – the right–left brain lore is one of the most widespread *neuromyths* in education (Goswami, 2004; Mason, 2009, p. 548). In mathematics education, the most common and most believed neuromyth is the idea of a *math person*. Many students, by middle school, firmly believe in the existence of math people. Those students interpret classroom experiences and grades as confirming evidence for a biological (and fixed) predisposition to struggle or do well in math. Decisions about postsecondary life and careers are made based on beliefs in the existence of math people.

Dominant narratives surrounding what is a math person shape most people's experiences and perception of mathematics. They control individuals' ability to develop relationship to math classrooms independent of or outside of the archetypical image of a *doer of mathematics*.

The idea of mathematics genes or success is rarely associated with groups of African or African American descent (e.g. Martin, 2009; Walker, 2012). Many scholars in the field of educational research have lamented the disproportionate number of studies focused on the failures of Black students. Martin (2009) argued that the abundance of data and the narrow focus on bridging the so-called race-based "achievement gap" have shored up existing and pervasive beliefs of a *racial hierarchy of mathematics ability* (p. 297). The idea that Asians and whites are on top of the math ability ladder and that African Americans are at the bottom is at the heart of most assumptions surrounding "what" and "who" is a math person.

Beliefs in the existence of a racial pyramid of academic ability are certainly not unique to mathematics. It is part of American history – it's in the DNA of the country's public education system. Government-funded public education has always been considered a controversial and divisive proposition

(Reese, 2000, pp. 20–21). Its inception, in the middle of the nineteenth century, was considered by many to be a necessary experiment. Dissenters viewed providing free education to white male teenagers living in poverty or from families who recently migrated to the United States as preposterous (p. 21). Ultimately, free public schools prevailed. They were promoted as the surest way to uphold and realize the, then, very young republic's democratic ideals and moral values. Values that never considered or extended to the liberation or education of enslaved school-aged children (p. 24). Values that, today, continue to label and treat Black children as antiintellectual, and that are the bedrock for the perception of a race-based hierarchy of math ability. Walker (2012) observed that images of "Blacks [and Brown teenagers] as physically gifted" juxtaposed to "Whites and Asians as intellectually so" are not only widely accepted, and often reproduced in mainstream American media, they also "diminish the importance of attending to [the] academic and intellectual selves" of urban youth of color (pp. 7–9). The assumptions about who can succeed in mathematics are rooted in a long and enduring American tradition: racism.

This ethnographic study made use of academic identity as a sense of *belonging* to show how a group of Black students developed their conception of mathematics and ensuing relationship to the discipline. Participants' stories of belonging made it possible to explore the limits and stunting effects of long-standing, yet understudied, assumptions surrounding mathematics and academic identity.

RACIAL INEQUALITY IN MATHEMATICS EDUCATION

This book joins in the conversation about mathematics as a high-status discipline, inequity in American education, and the impact that these two phenomena have had on racially and socially marginalized students. Beane (1989) characterized mathematics classrooms as "critical filters" that kept students of color and girls out of economic opportunities (see also Sells, 1973). More recently, a number of studies found that mathematics played "a pivotal role in the social structuring" of the lives of minority students living in underserved communities (Freitas, 2008, p. 43; see; Catsambis & Beveridge, 2001; Moses & Cobb, 2001). Mathematics has contributed to the exclusion of generations of Black Americans (and other racial minority groups) from certain economic opportunities and career paths. It will likely continue to preclude many more from ever imagining a future in STEM fields.

A motivator for this study is the well-documented relationship between students' performance in mathematics classroom and their economic prospects.

This relationship has received considerable attention in the last few decades, particularly since the rapid expansion of globalization, technology, and the subsequent ascension of mathematics to a high-status discipline necessary to compete in the job market.

However, it is important to note that debates about the state and future of mathematics education have been mostly about maintaining the country's world dominance (Gutstein, 2009, pp. 138–139). The problem with mathematics in the United States is usually framed as an imminent economic crisis. The fear of not producing enough "high-skilled" workers who can contribute to an increasingly more technological (thus mathematical) global labor market has been the biggest impetus for most reform initiatives in the field.

> *However, history shows that when U.S. productivity increases, the wealthiest benefit, not the majority. [Efforts] to channel public funding and students' talents into salvaging U.S. economic supremacy – in capital's interests – diametrically contrasts with educating youth to critique unjust relations of power and for democratic participation to change the world.*
>
> *(p. 138)*

The evolution of the field of mathematics education, in spite of calls for racial equity (e.g. NCTM, 1989, 2000), has been motivated by economic, geopolitical forces, and neoliberal (market-based) ideologies. Meanwhile, race-based inequality has persisted and is now a fixture, an accepted reality of the $K-12$ and higher mathematics education landscape.

PURPOSE

This book provides a counternarrative to the "dominant framings and story-lines about Black children and mathematics [that] have grown out of a race-comparative approach" (Martin, 2012, p. 48). It underscores the importance of the notion of "belonging" in educational research. Black and Brown students' voices and experiences are conspicuously absent in the field of mathematics education. Despite the abundance of empirical evidence of the factors adversely affecting academic performance, very little is known about those students' perception of mathematics, identification with the discipline, and interpretation of their classroom experiences (McGee, 2013, p. 255; see also; Ellington, 2006; Martin, 2006a, 2006b; Moody, 2003; Stinson, 2009).

Focusing on a group of honors students' perspectives of mathematics and interpretations of classroom experiences helped to unearth some of the visible and subliminal barriers that complicate the competence–confidence relationship for some students. Plato's "functionalist" or hierarchical model of education (Noddings, 1998) – a few students can and should be educated to rule while others are trained to serve – guides many scholarly and policy initiatives in education. This "ability model" has served to establish a "truth" around who is and what is mathematical; it has created an unexamined reality about STEM fields.

My hope is that this book highlights the dangers in propagating this notion that only a "few" are born and expected to succeed in mathematics. Ideas about the existence of a "math person" born with "near-supernatural" capacity for abstract thinking and sophisticated computations have helped to normalize racial differences in students' mathematics performance and attainment. Myths about a biological predisposition to succeed in mathematics continue America's racist history.

This study adds another dimension to the concept of a *growth mindset* – "the understanding that abilities and intelligence can be developed" (Dweck, 2006). Growth mindset has become ubiquitous among practitioners; it is widely accepted by educational researchers and psychologists (e.g. Boaler, 2016; Hochanadel & Finamore, 2015; Sheffield, 2017). It is now a fait accompli that a student's ability can be developed, regardless of the discipline. What about academic identity?

Like ability, I argue that positive academic identity can and should be fostered. Individuals' identification with a domain is not fixed. However, it requires ongoing justification and reaffirmation. Steele (1997) observed that individuals from social or racial groups characterized as "failures" in a particular discipline and who "remained identified with [the] domain" will experience sustained threats and obstacles to their continued "identification" (pp. 615–617). For some students, mathematics classrooms and activities present an ongoing threat and pressure; they are spaces and experiences imbued with the power to confirm or refute negative stereotypes about them.

> *High-achieving students are the most affected by stereotype threat and fare the worst when the condition of being stereotyped is presented. That is, students who are high achievement oriented, in terms of skill, motivation, and confidence, are the most impaired by stereotype threat. This threat is related to their efforts and frequent attempts to disconfirm these negative stereotypes and the academically harmful stress they cause.*
>
> (McGee, 2013, p. 257)

In the case of the students who participated in this study, being enrolled in honors precalculus and the prospects of having to take advanced college-level math courses represented a threat to their academic identity and a risk to their motivation to lead productive postsecondary lives.

This book provides in-service and prospective teachers the opportunity to examine the oppressive nature of mathematics as neutral and universal. *Exploring Identity as a Sense of Belonging* from northeast Philadelphia hopes to compel undergraduates, graduates, practitioners, and researchers to join or initiate movements aimed at countering narratives premised on the academic inferiority of certain groups. My hope is that this book foregrounds the need to redefine mathematics classrooms as antiracist projects and as sites where students can develop positive personal and academic identities.

OVERVIEW

The main arguments in this book are organized in seven chapters. They revolve around the "relationship between individual subjects and [their social realities] implicit" in the learning process and in their academic identity development (Hardy, 2007, p. 23).

I open with Oxford High School, its history, and story. Chapter 1 shows how Oxford and its honors students are part of the *urban education tale* – a tale wherein Black and Brown families and their public schools are constructed and only understood as part of a "culture of poverty." This section of the book serves as context with which to understand what it meant for this study's participants to continually engage in making sense of being "good" promising students in a "failing" school.

Then, the focus narrows to the classroom and Ms. Turner, the lead teacher of the honors precalculus class. I explain how her extensive experience in teaching in underresourced, racially, and socioeconomically segregated public schools helps to examine the interplay between perceptions of urban public schools, their students, and existing race-based beliefs that pervade mathematics education. Chapter 2 cautions against fixed and rigid ideas about the "ideal" learner and how they can distort and limit even well-intentioned and competent teachers' expectations of students.

The subsequent sections, Chapters 3 and 4, take a close and careful look at students' beliefs about "what" and "who" is a math person and the role those beliefs played in their math identity construction. Like most students around the world, the 11 teenage boys and girls interviewed for this study learned to accept the myth of a math person as someone born with near-supernatural abilities. But, they were also taught to expect math people to be Asian or white males. I show how assumptions about math genes and widespread beliefs of a racial hierarchy of math ability combine to complicate, and in some instances, stunt participants' ability to make sense of their $K - 12$ mathematics education.

The voices, stories, and experiences used in this book make clear some of the limitations of theories and frameworks based on the presupposed link between classroom success and academic identity. Chapter 5 expands on the idea of identity as belonging. It provides the framework and rationale with which to fully understand how students developed their conception of mathematics education and ensuing relationship to the discipline.

Chapter 6 provides an overview of the history of mathematics education in the United States. It shows how standards aimed at addressing the underrepresentation of Black and Brown people in STEM oversimplified and potentially undermined "the complexities of race, minority/marginalized status, underachievement" (Martin, 2003, p. 10). I explain how mathematics education's claim to neutrality and roots in neoliberal ideals prevented a century-old battle over content and pedagogy to effect meaningful changes in addressing existing racial disparities in the field.

This book not only brings much needed awareness to mathematics classrooms' potential to perpetuate or reverse the persistence of inequity in America's public school system but also calls for a reckoning.

REFERENCES

Beane, B. D. (1989). Mathematics and science: Critical filters for the future of minority students. In National Research Council (Ed.), *Making mathematics work for minorities: Proceedings of the region I workshop (1989)*. Washington, DC: The National Academies Press. doi:10.17226/19072

Boaler, J. (2016). *Mathematical mindsets: Unleashing students' potential through creative math, inspiring messages and innovative teaching*. San Francisco, CA: Jossey-Bass.

Catsambis, S., & Beveridge, A. A. (2001). Neighborhood and school influences on the family life and mathematics performance eight-grade students. *Center for Research on the Education of Students Placed at Risk*, *54*, 1–30.

Dweck, C. S. (2006). *Mindset: The new psychology of success*. New York, NY: Ballantine Books.

Ellington, R. (2006). *Having their say: High-achieving African-American mathematics majors discuss the family, educational, communal and personal factors that impacted their decision to succeed and persist in mathematics.* Unpublished doctoral dissertation, University of Maryland, College.

Freitas, E. D. (2008). Troubling teacher identity: Preparing mathematics teachers to teach for diversity. *Teaching Education, 19*(1), 43–55.

Goswami, U. (2004). Neuroscience and education. *British Journal of Educational Psychology, 74*, 1–14.

Gutstein, E. (2009). The politics of mathematics education in the US: Dominant and counter agendas. In B. Greer, S. Mukhopadhyay, A. B. Powell, & S. Nelson-Barber (Eds.), *Culturally responsive mathematics education* (pp. 137–164). New York, NY: Routledge.

Hardy, T. (2007). Participation and performance: Keys to confident learning in mathematics? *Research in Mathematics Education, 9*(1), 21–32.

Hochanadel, A., & Finamore, D. (2015). Fixed and growth mindset in education and how grit helps students persist in the face of adversity. *Journal of International Education Research, 11*(1), 47–50.

Martin, D. B. (2003). Hidden assumptions and unaddressed questions in mathematics for all in rhetoric. *Mathematics Educator, 13*(2), 7–21.

Martin, D. B. (2006a). Mathematics learning and participation as racialized forms of experience: African American parents speak on the struggle for mathematics literacy. *Mathematical Thinking and Learning, 8*, 197–229.

Martin, D. B. (2006b). Mathematics learning and participation in African American context: The co-construction of identity in two intersecting realms of experience. In N. Nasir & P. Cobb (Eds.), *Diversity, equity, and access to mathematical ideas* (pp. 146–158). New York, NY: Teachers College Press.

Martin, D. B. (2009). Researching race in mathematics education. *Teachers College Record, 111*(2), 295–338.

Martin, D. B. (2012). Learning mathematics while Black. *Educational Foundations, 26*, 47–66.

Mason, L. (2009). Bridging neuroscience and education: A two-way path is possible. *Cortex, 45*, 548–549.

McGee, E. (2013). Young, black, mathematically gifted, and stereotyped. *The High School Journal*, *96*(3), 253–263.

Moody, V. (2003). The ins and outs of succeeding in mathematics: African American students' notions and perceptions. *Multicultural Perspectives*, *5*(1), 33–37.

Moses, R. P., & Cobb, C. E. (2001). *Radical equations: Civil rights from Mississippi to the algebra project*. Boston, MA: Beacon Press.

National Council of Teachers of Mathematics. (1989). *Curriculum and evaluation standards for school mathematics*. Reston, VA: Author.

National Council of Teachers of Mathematics. (2000). *Principles and standards for school mathematics*. Reston, VA: Author.

Noddings, N. (1998). *Philosophy of education*. Boulder, CO: Westview Press.

Reese, W. J. (2000). Public schools and the elusive search for the common good. In L. Cuban & D. Shipps (Eds.), *Reconstructing the common good in education: Coping with intractable American dilemmas* (pp. 13–31). Palo Alto, CA: Stanford University Press.

Sells, L. W. (1973). High school mathematics as the critical filter in the job market. In *Proceedings of the conference on minority graduate education*. Berkeley, CA: University of California.

Sheffield, L. J. (2017). Dangerous myths about "gifted" students. *Journal of ZDM Mathematics Education*, *49*, 13–23.

Steele, C. M. (1997). A threat in the air: How stereotypes shape intellectual identity and performance. *American Psychologist*, *52*(6), 613–629.

Stinson, D. (2009). Negotiating sociocultural discourses: The counter-storytelling of academically mathematically successful African American male students. In D. Martin (Ed.), *Mathematics teaching, learning, and liberation in the lives of black children* (pp. 265–288). London: Routledge.

Walker, E. N. (2012). *Building mathematics learning communities: Improving outcomes in urban high schools*. New York, NY: Teachers College Press.

1

OXFORD HIGH SCHOOL: AN URBAN EDUCATION TALE

My first time visiting Oxford High School, I was sure to have driven to the wrong address. The grass along the perimeter was overgrown and unkempt. The front entrance was deserted – it was rarely used during the 2015–16 academic year. I searched through my phone for an explanation. It struck me, in that moment, that I could be standing before another casualty of recent waves of shortsighted educational policies (e.g. Race to the Top). Policies that, too often, resulted in school closures and not much else. It was the correct address. The massive mock renaissance building, sitting conspicuously on more than 1,000 square feet, stayed clear of the *turnaround* movement that was sweeping through the nation. Oxford did not experience the "little pain and discomfort" purported to be necessary to reform "low-performing" urban school districts like Philadelphia (Johnson, 2012).

The focus of this chapter is on understanding the "contexts" in which this study's participants developed their math identities. Making sense of race-based differences in academic performance is not confined to the classroom, nor can it be defined only in terms of "gaps" in disciplinary practices or content knowledge. I contend that racial inequality in the field of mathematics exists and has persisted, in large part, because schools are reflections and extensions of the unequal societies that create them. Schools are "sites where identities are produced," get reproduced (Urrieta, 2007, p. 108), and where existing social norms are reified.

Schools are not neutral sites. They are political and value-laden institutions. They always have. The classroom or the learning that happens within its four walls has never been impervious or immune to sociohistorical ills (e.g. racism, sexism, classism). James Baldwin (1963), one of the leading voices on racial injustice in the twentieth century, argued, quite pointedly, that "Education does not and cannot occur in a vacuum. It occurs in a social context and it has social ends."

This chapter centers on Oxford High School, a comprehensive secondary school in the district of Philadelphia. I open with a description of Oxford and a brief historical account of public schools in urban districts. I argue that Oxford, in many ways, is the epitome of popular and long-standing beliefs of urban schools as "failures" and "undesirable"; as part of a "culture of poverty" where both schools and the large percentage of kids of color enrolled in them are "so dysfunctional that they do not know how to operate in mainstream society" (Ladson-Billings, 2017, p. 81; see Lewis, 1966; Moynihan, 1965; Payne, 2005).

This *urban education tale*, this conventional wisdom about "who" attends and "what" it means to enroll in schools like Oxford, has eclipsed, from our imagination and national debates, the real, complex, and multilayered stories of Black students' experiences with academic learning. Students who graduate from schools like Oxford and go on to lead productive lives are often depicted as "survivors" or "gritty." Their "grit" is used to reduce others, *pushed* or *pulled* out of school (Jordan, Lara, & McPartland, 1996; see Fine, 1991), as simply victims or "lazy."

This chapter shows how this urban education tale limited and distorted a group of students' perception and relationship to classroom successes. I end with a caution against fixed and narrow conceptions of the "ideal" student which, in this study, combines with America's history of fear and contempt for urban schools to constrain and "regulate" the math identities of very motivated and promising students.

AN URBAN EDUCATION TALE

Everyone entered Oxford through a nondescript back entrance. From across a narrow and quiet two-way street, the permanent presence of large dumpsters made it hard to see the entryway, or for an onlooker to think of it as a main entrance. In the spring, there were often sizable puddles of stagnant waters scattered about the lawn. During the warmer months of the school year, clusters of construction workers mixed in with teachers and other staff members were often seen chatting and smoking near parked trucks. Long before dismissal, the usual ebb and flow of students strolling through pockets of adults enjoying their lunch or on cigarette break added another layer of unsettled energy about the back entrance. Often, I would cross the lightly trafficked street at a pace nearly slower than that of the students. I would continue at the same slow pace through the adults lazing around, through the dumpsters, and the metal detectors. Each time, eyes and ears pried open, I tried to catch pieces of the latest school gossip that could help my understanding of the daily and symbolic reality of attending Oxford High School.

There was nothing inviting about the building's back entrance. Nor was there anything inspiring or welcoming about Oxford's welcome area:

> *I was greeted by the same older White officer. He was polite, but indifferent. I emptied the content of my pockets into a basket. I walked through the metal detectors to the waiting and welcoming room. It was spacious, but mostly bare. There were adults, presumably parents or guardians, sometimes accompanied by students, and sometimes not, waiting, on the other side of the metal detectors. It was a waiting room with nowhere to wait or sit. There was often a small group congregated before a rectangular folding table manned by a staff member responsible for late passes and student Ids. No one ever seemed eager or interested to be there.*
>
> *(Field Notes, 1/15/2016)*

I wondered, many times during the course of this study, what a morning routine of overgrown grass, puddles, dumpsters, and other markers of institutional neglect had on a student's academic identity. How did metal detectors, armed security officers, dim hallways, and gated windows make this study's participants and the larger Oxford student community – 57% Black and 33% Latinx – feel about schooling, their academic prospects, and themselves? Was Oxford, to them, an extension (and affirmation) of popular depiction and treatment of Black and Latinx teenagers as uninterested in school, prone to violence, and "commonly engaged in criminal behavior" (Walker, 2012, p. 7)?

Oxford High School was built in first decade of the twentieth century to educate kids of white-working class families (Fig. 1.1). About 100 years later, the school now represents the "typical" characterization of public schools in urban districts. Located in a northeast section of Philadelphia, Oxford received an overall performance grade of 1 out of 10 at the end of the 2015–2016 academic year. The school is in an underresourced neighborhood with a median income below that of Philadelphia. Only 11% of Oxford's students scored proficient or better in their algebra in Pennsylvania Keystone Exams that year. And even though violence had been on the decline in Philadelphia's public schools for a few years before this study, the number of "serious incidents" involving "weapons" and "assault" at Oxford remained stubbornly high compared to the district's average (see Table 1.1).

Fig. 1.1. Oxford High School, 1916. Digital Collections, Free Library of Philadelphia. Retrieved from https://libwww.freelibrary.org/digital/item/ 2699.

Table 1.1. Excerpt from Oxford High School's 2015–16 Serious Incidents Reports.

Serious Incidents	Oxford	District Average
Assaults	36	4.8
Drug and alcohol offenses	15	1.1
Disorderly conduct	44	10.7
Weapons	15	1.8

Source: The School District of Philadelphia and The Office of Safe Schools Advocate (OSSA).

This was just a snapshot of data; an all too familiar biased selection of facts that stems from and reinforces long-held beliefs of urban schools as "failures." State exams' scores, incidence rate of violence, the educational level, and socioeconomic status of the community surrounding a school constitute the breadth and depth of information most commonly used to evaluate schools and their students. This incomplete and, in my view misuse of, data represent the basis for many families, privileged to choose, to leave the district. It informs school policies, practices, and often shapes teachers' attitudes toward students; it allows for the propagation and legitimation of urban public schools as sinking ships. The pervasive narrative of schools, like Oxford, as "a malignant force to be ignored if you can or snuffed out altogether" (Ewing, 2018, p. 1) has become so commonplace in national conversations about public education that there seems to be no space in our imaginations and political machinations for reform approaches other than school closures.

Even though Oxford escaped the latest round of neoliberal and market-based initiatives disguised as educational reform (Lipman, 2011), the school, its students, and teaching workforce have not broken free of our history of "contempt" for urban public schools. Our deep-seated fear of teenagers of color, the overwhelming majority of students in school districts like Philadelphia, continues to be a constitutive aspect of mainstream perception of urban schools.

> *On my way back to my car parked on [...] street, I spotted the other doctoral student responsible for the honor's English classes – by then, he had been working with this study's participants for about two years. He was smoking a cigarette in front of [...] building. It was bitterly cold that day. We greeted each other. He proceeded almost immediately to tell me about a "riot" – his wording – that happened at Oxford, the day before, where 6 students were arrested. This was unprompted, but not unprecedented. During one of our first meetings, the summer before the 2015-16 school year, he warned me of how "chaotic" and "crazy" Oxford was and how I should brace myself for the worst.*
>
> *(Field Notes, Wed 01/20/2016)*

Ten months of observational notes and hundreds of pages of interview transcripts showed no evidence of violence or violent incidents among the students observed for this book; nor did I experience or personally witness any violent acts during the 2015–16 academic year. Students were generally cooperative and receptive of the classroom's rules of conduct and academic demands. In fact, both student teachers – Mr. Bond and Mr. London – who assisted the lead teacher during the Fall 2015 and Spring 2016 semesters, respectively, were "pleasantly surprised" (excerpted from Mr. London's interview) by how well students responded to them. This is not to suggest that there were no violent incidents at Oxford that year. There were, and, as mentioned earlier, they far exceeded the district average in every category.

However, I argue that the 25 to 30 honors students observed for this book were learning and doing mathematics, and presumably English and Language Arts, in a classroom atmosphere unlike and perhaps shielded from the larger culture of school violence. So, for me, the important question was: why the warning?

The warning was probably intended as help and guidance. It was surely meant to ease my transition and expedite my understanding of what it means to work at Oxford. My counterpart, a white male in his late twenties, who was further along in his doctoral studies, worked with the same group of honors students in English and Language Arts. He had been working at Oxford for about two years when I met him. He was very familiar with this study's participants. He genuinely cared for them – he knew all of them as juniors and had spent the previous academic year helping them with their college essays and applications. So, his warning about how "crazy" and "chaotic" Oxford was and no mention of the honors students (or their achievements) with whom he spent most of his time was a bit puzzling.

> *Educators who deal with the urban are constructed as sophisticated,*
> *but the urban students and families themselves are not.*
> *(Leonardo & Hunter, 2007, p. 782)*

Leonardo and Hunter's (2007) analysis of the term "urban" as a "signifier" used and commodified to connote diversity and sophistication (p. 782) helped to untangle part of that puzzle for me. In the midst of mainstream movements to promote diversity and embrace inclusion – this includes recent corporate endorsements, and likely hollowing or sanitizing, of the *Black Lives Matter* movement – it is important to underscore that urban communities of color and their school-aged children are rarely considered "sophisticated." Unsophisticated and uncultured is how most of us think of them. Meanwhile, teachers, researchers, educational leaders, and institutions working with or in urban spaces are, by default, depicted and positioned – some position themselves – as "saviors," progressive-minded, and "cutting edge" (p. 782).

The warning, to me, was more than just guidance. It is in line with the history of contempt and fear that can only envision and always assumes the worst of urban public schools and their students. It is part of the urban education tale always eager and proud to inflict "a little pain and discomfort" to the presumed "crazy" and "chaotic" lives of families of color living in certain urban neighborhoods. The warning is rooted in a set of beliefs that leave no room to consider what schools like Oxford and its students can offer; no space to imagine or foster interest in the 11 rich and sophisticated stories that made this book possible.

The fact that "urban school districts that primarily serve students of color [are] viewed with pity and contempt" (Ewing, 2018, p. 2) has limited and contaminated our ability to adequately evaluate urban public school's performance and importance to a community; it has flattened and devalued Black and Latinx teenagers' experiences and voices in mainstream explanations about academic performance; it has contributed to, and in some instances, exacerbated, the history of socioeconomic and racial isolation of underserved communities of color.

A BRIEF URBAN EDUCATION HISTORY

Oxford's academic performance and its characterization as "failing" are the result of decades of government-funded residential segregation and socioeconomic oppression that left many American urban districts stuck with issues like unemployment, concentration of poverty, and crime.

> *Our system of official segregation was not the result of a single law that consigned African Americans to designated neighborhoods. Rather, scores of racially explicit laws, regulations, and government practices combined to create nationwide system of urban ghettos, surrounded by white suburbs. Private discrimination also played a role, but it would have been considerably less effective had it not been embraced and reinforced by [the] government.*
>
> *(Rothstein, 2017, p. XII)*

A mass exodus of more affluent and disproportionally white families from urban districts, commonly referred to as "white flight," followed the 1954 Brown V. Board of Education decision. Laws separating students based on race were struck down; they were deemed unconstitutional. The migration of middle- and upper-income families (including Black families) to the suburbs severely weakened the "tax base of city governments and school systems" (Rury, 2005, p. 7). Large numbers of African Americans from the South, escaping more racist southern cities and in search of better economic opportunities, moved to northern and urban districts like Philadelphia throughout most of the twentieth century. White flight, the influx of Black southern families into urban centers, and the string of racist federally funded policies that followed (e.g. redlining, urban renewal) combined to create a concentration of poverty and the formation of cities or urban spaces with mostly Black American residents (Wilson, 2009). These factors left many neighborhoods, like the community surrounding Oxford High School, trapped in "deteriorating physical condition and [with] substandard schools" for many generations (p. 567).

Indeed, Oxford High School and its surrounding community are still reeling from the devastating and enduring impact of government-sponsored explicit and implicit racist policies from the previous century. Oxford's story, like the story of many other public schools in Philadelphia serving predominantly low-income families of color, is America's story, an abundance of wealth and opportunities entangled in a history of systemic injustice and racial inequity. It's the story of democratic and meritocratic ideals melded with institutionalized racism and gatekeeping forces that, often, blame the individual, their communities, and a "culture of poverty" for being and feeling left out of the American dream.

This study's participants were tasked with making sense of success in a "dysfunctional," "failing," and undesirable school. They were to cultivate positive relationships with academic learning while living in communities and identifying with social groups that have historically been characterized and treated as anti-education and culturally inferior. Students were to figure out ways to develop a sense of belonging to a community of practice, a high-status discipline, and exclusive tradition that prides itself on being accessible to a selected few "geniuses" – white and Asian males.

> *African American students face challenges unique to them as students in American schools at all levels by virtue of their social identity as African Americans and of the way that identity can be a source of devaluation in contemporary American society.... contemporary conversation about African-American achievement ignores these social facts in ways that seriously distort the debate.*
>
> *(Perry, Steele, & Hilliard, 2003, p. vii)*

Debates over the purpose, future of public schools, and disagreements about what access to quality education means have persisted and continue to influence today's attitudes, policies, and politics. However, it is worth noting that publicly funded K–12 schools have always functioned as laboratories and marketing tools for the American ethos: "individuals could overcome disadvantage through hard work and application" (Reese, 2000, p. 24). This narrow conception of schools as meritocratic silos has clouded our understanding of the historical relevance and sociocultural impact of the spaces where students are learning.

Schools' history of creating, reinforcing, or exacerbating inequities, and the classroom's role in shaping individuals' self-concepts, relationships to their communities and to the world around them are necessary contexts and frameworks in thinking about and making sense of student's academic identity development. Martin (2000) offered a fitting illustration of this. He showed how combining "the sociohistorical and present-day mathematical experiences" of a group of Black boys and that of their families allowed space to develop nuanced and meaningful insights about the friction that exists between students' personal identities and the *normative identity of a doer of mathematics* (pp. 19–20).

Studying how students stitched together aspects of their history, personal stories, and individual journeys in math classrooms to figure whether they can or want to belong to the exclusive community of math people is, or at least ought to be, an integral part of addressing racial inequality in mathematics education.

"STRAIGHT A'S? YOU LYING"

Nigel: Why do people think I'm not like a school person. Alright, last year, when I got my report card, I got straight A's. So, I'm walking down the hallway, a teacher said: "let me see your report card, you probably got D's and C's."

Researcher: Was that a teacher you had before?

Nigel: No.

Researcher: He doesn't even know you?

Nigel: Don't know me. He took my report card, "straight A's? You lying." I'm like it's right there. Like, dude really [italics added for emphasis] couldn't believe I had straight A's.

Researcher: Does that bother you?

Nigel: Yeah, it bothers me. I don't even know why.

It took a while before Nigel and I bonded. In the first few weeks, he wouldn't really talk to me; he refused my help. It did not matter if he was struggling with a particular problem, or was in need of quick clarification or refresher, he would always wait for Ms. Turner. I asked him about it. He replied that I probably thought that he was "dumb." Nigel did not provide any explanation for why he felt that way; nor was he able to recall any moment where I said or did anything that suggested that he was "dumb."

Even in the face of clear and undisputable evidence, like Nigel's report card, this study's participants had to grapple with ongoing tension and negotiations between their evolving self-concepts and a *designated identity*, a tradition that formulates, and even regulates, what/who is a "good" or "smart" student

(Sfard & Prusak, 2005, p. 18). Nigel had to contend with why his report card was not proof that he was a "school person." He had to reconcile classroom successes to enduring narratives that never considered him. He had to engage daily and continually in the formulation and articulation of belonging, of being part of a tradition that is typically derogatory of Black and Brown boys.

The fixed image of the "ideal student" and its exclusionary effect is not unique to the U.S. Others have documented and analyzed its adverse impact on students of color in the United Kingdom, Australia, Canada, and other countries (e.g. Gillborn & Youdell, 2000; Ibrahim, 1999; Youdell, 2003, 2006). Ibrahim's (1999) ethnographic study of a group of Senegalese students studying English in a Canadian school is a fitting example. He showed how students, from a region, nationality, and culture different from that of African Americans, were "expected to be Black, act Black and so be the marginalized Other" (p. 353; see Hall, 1991; hooks, 1992).

Consistent with some of the studies referenced above, this study's participants were also expected and constructed to be "the marginalized Other." For some in the honors precalculus class, like Nigel, this meant a never-ending process of convincing the adults in their lives and themselves that they too could "fit" our narrow conception of an "ideal student" (Youdell, 2003).

The students observed for this book were among the roughly third of American high school students enrolled in precalculus nationwide. In fact, some were part of the "10% [to] complete the sequence of high school mathematics – algebra, geometry, trigonometry, and pre-calculus" before college (McGee & Martin, 2011, p. 48). This was also true of their academic achievements relative to the majority of Oxford's student population. While the school graduated only 60% of its seniors at the end of the 2015–16 academic year, every student in Ms. Turner's class had fulfilled their credit requirements for graduation long before the deadline. In fact, most of seniors in the college pipeline were accepted in a college or were finalizing their decisions months before the end of this study. Moreover, Oxford's 2016 valedictorian – the senior with the highest grades in their cohort, the prom king – student voted by peers as the most popular face of their graduating class and one of the finalists of the school district's annual science fair were all seniors in the classroom observed for this study.

In the midst of mainstream beliefs about the complexity and intractability of the issues plaguing urban school districts in America, this study's participants are the "resilient children," often left out of mainstream educational research, who persevere and succeed in spite of the systemic and persistent failures of their institutions and government (Borman & Rachuba, 2001, p. 2; see Finn & Rock, 1997).

However, the cumulative impact of occurrences, like the excerpt cited above, where students like Nigel are routinely seen as "intrinsically anti-school" and antiintellectual (Youdell, 2003, p. 15), puts a caveat on participants' classroom successes. Scholastic achievements became imbued with meanings that went beyond, and in some instances, overshadowed, ability and potential. Academic learning for this study's participants, especially in mathematics classrooms, was racialized forms of experiences where participation and identification involved "developing competencies related to [a] discipline and 'a way of being in the world' relative to the discipline" (Valeras, Martin, & Kane, 2012, p. 324).

OXFORD IS NOT A "SPECIAL ADMISSION SCHOOL"

It was commonplace to hear students, including this study's participants, complain or express genuine regrets about having spent their secondary education at Oxford High School. Some were still hopeful that they could transfer out:

> ...an 11th grader in honor's math wanted to transfer to a charter school. She believed that Oxford was "bad" because kids were having sex in the basement instead of going to class. She told me that there was a kid "who [took] dumps on the staircase" leading to the basement. I told her that I didn't know that there was a basement — no one else ever mentioned or corroborated her story.
>
> (Field Notes, 02/12/2016)

Whether Oxford students were engaged in the behaviors mentioned above is inconsequential. The critical point here is that students were interpreting fairly typical adolescent indiscretions (e.g. underage drinking, cutting class) as evidence that they were trapped in a place filled with "bad" kids. Likewise, singular and isolated events – the student purported to be defecating in public, an institutional failure to accommodate a student with possible learning or physical differences – were used to perpetuate the lore of urban public schools as "dumps" that enroll a specific "type" of students. The 11th grader quoted above, although unprompted, provided what she considered to be indefensible examples of Oxford's perverse and toxic overall culture. She provided, in her mind, irrefutable evidence for why she, and everyone else privileged enough to choose, should leave.

This perception of Oxford as a place reserved for "discarded" school-aged children whom the district of Philadelphia "didn't need" seeped into the academic identity of the honors students interviewed for this book.

Shalik: It might be the area that I live in.

Researcher: But you're an honor's class, you don't think you should be like "there are bunch of math geniuses in [my] class?"

Shalik: Yeah, I do but it's not the case. I kinda feel like...you know that this school is not like special admission so, I feel like they wanna have the honor's class, they have to use the kids that they can. That's what I think.

This was excerpted from Shalik's first interview. He and other participants rejected being enrolled in honors courses as any indication or a measure of their academic ability. He conceded, later in the interview, that the honors precalculus class was exceedingly more challenging than the "regular math classes" at Oxford which he characterized as "very, very easy." And in spite of his good grades in the class, Shalik was convinced that he and other seniors in were "unsure when it comes to math."

De facto segregation, racial separation caused by individuals' or groups' actions, has not only widened race-based divisions in American schools but also distorted the self-concept and academic identity of students enrolled in schools like Oxford. A 15-year-old girl interviewed for Kozol's (2005) study of school resegregation offered a powerful, painfully vivid, and still relevant description of the impact of *apartheid* schooling on some students:

> *It's as if you've been put in a garage...[like] they don't have room for something but aren't sure if they should throw it out, they put it there where they don't need to think of it again.*
>
> (p. 28)

In participants' eyes, a history of academic success at Oxford was indicative of nothing. Tamika, considered by teachers and her peers as one of the most studious in her cohort, was extremely concerned about her future. She was accepted to several colleges but was convinced that she was unprepared and unfit for the rigor and exigencies of college. Tamika felt similarly about her fellow classmates; she even dismissed the fact that her good friend, Weldon, was Oxford's valedictorian. She thought that it was meaningless and just the end result of teachers helping students during class exams.

Being the highest performer of Oxford's 2015–16 graduating class bore no real significance to many of this study's participants, including Weldon, the valedictorian. In fact, participants attributed it all, including their recruitment into the college pipeline, to widespread nepotism, and suspected grade inflation:

> *...a handful of seniors were enjoying their lunch in the classroom and discussing their anxieties and excitements about prom. Someone mentioned the valedictorian. Another student responded that "people [were] quick to brag about grades" that they didn't really get on their own. She warned that honor's students were going to be in for a rough awakening in college. None of the students objected.*
>
> *(Field Notes, Thur 05/26/16)*

Inflated grades are not unique to Oxford or public K–12 schools. Grade inflation is pervasive in education, particularly in higher education (Jewell, McPherson, & Tieslau, 2013). What is peculiar here is a group of students, with a history of classroom success, who developed self-concepts and academic identities constrained and tainted by what Oxford High School symbolizes to them and their community.

Participants not only dismissed their history of academic successes but also struggled seeing one another without or beyond the urban education tale. Most of the students in Ms. Turner class had been part of the college pipeline program for two years; they spent at least half of their secondary education enrolled in the same honors mathematics and English classes. They were Oxford's highest performers and least expected to "misbehave" or cause "trouble." Nonetheless, the pervasiveness and perniciousness tale of Black and Brown teenagers as "dangerous" or culturally inferior clouded participants' evaluation of themselves and of one another.

> *Cultural racism – the cultural images and messages that affirmed the assumed superiority of Whites and the assumed inferiority of people of color – is like smog air. Sometimes it is so thick it is visible, other times it less apparent, but always, day and day out, we are breathing it.*
>
> *(Tatum, 2017, p. 86)*

This "smog air" was evidenced in participants' interview transcripts and documented interactions with classmates. For instance, Tamika was extremely concerned about her future and was careful not to engage in anything or befriend anyone that could jeopardize her chances at realizing her dreams. I never observed her talk or joke with Nigel or Andre. She stayed clear of most

Oxford students who, in her eyes, did not appear to take school seriously enough – she was close to Weldon, the school valedictorian, with whom she drove to and from school. Tamika viewed many students, including some of her classmates in honors precalculus, as threats to her chances at a successful postsecondary life.

Each participant received a letter in their junior year at Oxford that begins with "Congratulations on your acceptance into the [college pipeline] program"; a program designed to enrich the learning experiences of students who have demonstrated a sustained level of academic success, good classroom behavior, and attendance in their first two years of high school. However, students were certain that unearned grades were the primary reason for their selection into the program. Having Oxford's valedictorian as a classmate constituted further evidence of institutionally accepted and expected academic cheating. Like the characterization of typical teenage behaviors as markers of a "bad" school, students overestimated the role that grade inflation played in their secondary education's success and in their recruitment into honors courses because it did not fit the narrative of contempt and fear that they've been taught and have internalized about their school, their community, and themselves. Being an Oxford student, in their minds, was the most reliable appraisal of their academic potential; it was the best predictor of their presumed limited postsecondary prospects and future. They were recommended to the honors precalculus because schools like Oxford that wish to have honors classes could only "use the kids they had."

CONCLUSION

In this chapter, I have shown the importance of schools, as sites with a history and a story, in seeking to understand and discuss students' academic identity. Participants' relationship to schooling, their interpretation of classroom experiences, and their identification with mathematics developed within the rigid boundaries of America's *social imaginary* – the range of possible identities available to a group in a society (Ibrahim, 1999, p. 351). The racial and socioeconomic isolation of Oxford High School and its surrounding urban community of color erected in students' consciousness a fixed and stunted conception of their potential and prospects. The range of possible identities offered to them at Oxford, in their communities, and in America precluded this study's participants from embodying and internalizing their history of classroom success as an essential dimension of their academic identity.

This book, based on a purposeful sampling of resilient Black teenage boys and girls, illustrates the pernicious impact of institutional racism and racial inequity on academically motivated students. Theories and frameworks based on the presupposed link between competence and academic confidence, in the case of this study's participants, are simply inadequate and incomplete. The college pipeline program provided honors students an educational experience and resources superior than that of other Oxford students. However, Ernst and Young and Cecil B. Moore University's partnership could not inoculate them from pervasive racist ideologies enmeshed in education and mathematics. The honors program was not successful in protecting students' academic identity development against the existence and persistence of the urban education tale; participants' classroom successes did not shield them from our fear and perception of Black and Brown adolescents, in school districts like Philadelphia, as academically inferior and part of a culture of depravity.

REFERENCES

Baldwin, J. (1963). "Living and growing in a white world," radio recording. Retrieved from https://www.youtube.com/watch?v=QWF2Wjic7Vs

Borman, G. D., & Rachuba, L. T. (2001). Academic success among poor and minority students: An analysis of competing models of school effects. *Center for Research on the Education of Students Placed At Risk (CRESPAR)*, *52*, 1–36. Retrieved from www.csos.jhu.edu

Ewing, E. (2018). *Ghosts in the schoolyard: Racism and school closings on Chicago's south side*. Chicago, IL: University of Chicago Press.

Fine, M. (1991). *Framing dropouts: Notes on the politics of an urban public high school*. Albany, NY: State University of New York Press.

Finn, J. D., & Rock, D. A. (1997). Academic success among students at risk for school failure. *Journal of Applied Psychology*, *82*, 221–234.

Gillborn, D., & Youdell, D. (2000). *Rationing education: Policy, practice, reform and equity*. Buckingham: Open University Press.

Hall, S. (1991). Ethnicity: Identity and difference. *Radical America*, *13*(4), 9–20.

hooks, b. (1992). *Black looks*. Boston, MA: South End Press.

Ibrahim, A. E. K. M. (1999). Becoming black: Rap and hip hop, race, gender, identity, and the politics of ESL learning. *TESOL Quarterly*, *33*(3), 349–369.

Jewell, R. T., McPherson, M. A., & Tieslau, M. A. (2013). Whose fault is it? Assigning blame for grade inflation in higher education. *Applied Economics, 45*, 1185–1200.

Johnson, A. W. (2012). "Turnaround" as shock therapy: Race, neoliberalism, and school reform. *Urban Education, 48*(2), 232–256. doi: 10.1177/0042085912441941

Jordan, W. J., Lara, J., & McPartland, J. M. (1996). Exploring the causes of early dropout among race-ethnic and gender groups. *Youth & Society, 28*(1), 62–94. doi:10.1177/0044118X96028001003

Kozol, J. (2005). *The shame of the nation: The restoration of apartheid schooling in America.* New York, NY: Crown Publishers.

Ladson-Billings, G. (2017). "Makes me wanna holler": Refuting the "culture of poverty" discourse in urban schooling. *The Annals of the American Academy of Political and Social Science, 673*(1), 80–90. doi:10.1177/0002716217718793

Leonardo, Z., & Hunter, M. (2007). Imagining the urban: The politics of race, class, and schooling. In W. T. Pink & G. W. Noblit (Eds.), *International handbook of urban education* (pp. 779–802). Dordrecht: Springer.

Lewis, O. (1966). The culture of poverty. *Scientific American, 215*(4), 19–25.

Lipman, P. (2011). *The new political economy of urban education: Neoliberalism, race, and the Right to the city.* New York, NY: Taylor & Francis.

Martin, D. B. (2000). *Mathematics success and failure among African-American youth: The roles of sociohistorical context, community forces, school influence, and individual agency.* New York, NY: Routledge.

McGee, E. O., & Martin, D. B. (2011). From the hood to being hooded: Case study of a Black male PhD. *Journal of African American Males in Education, 2*(1), 46–65.

Moynihan, D. P. (1965). *The Negro family: The case for national action.* Washington, DC: Office of Policy Planning and Research, United States Department of Labor. Government Printing Office.

Payne, R. (2005). *A framework for understanding poverty* (4th revised ed.). Highlands, TX: Aha! Process.

Perry, T., Steele, C., & Hilliard, A. G. (2003). *Young, gifted, and black: Promoting high achievement among African-American students.* Boston, MA: Beacon Press.

Reese, W. J. (2000). Public schools and the elusive search for the common good. In L. Cuban & D. Shipps (Eds.), *Reconstructing the common good in education: Coping with intractable American dilemmas* (pp. 13–31). Palo Alto, CA: Stanford University Press.

Rothstein, R. (2017). *The color of law : A forgotten history of how our government segregated America* (1st ed.). New York, NY: Liveright Publishing Corporation.

Rury, J. L. (2005). Introduction: The changing social contours of urban education. In J. L. Rury (Ed.), *Urban education in the United States: A historical reader* (pp. 1–12). New York, NY: Palgrave MacMillan.

Sfard, A., & Prusak, A. (2005). Telling identities: In search of an analytical tool for investigating learning as a culturally shaped activity. *Educational Researcher, 34*(4), 14–22.

Tatum, B. D. (2017). *"Why are all the Black kids sitting together in the cafeteria?" and other conversations about race.* New York, NY: Basic Books.

Urrieta, L., Jr (2007). Identity production in figured worlds: How some Mexican Americans become Chicana/o activist educators. *The Urban Review, 39*(2), 117–144. doi:10.1007/s11256-007-0050-1

Valeras, M., Martin, D. B., & Kane, J. M. (2012). Content learning and identity construction: A framework to strengthen African American students' mathematics and science learning in urban elementary schools. *Human Development, 55,* 319–339.

Walker, E. N. (2012). *Building mathematics learning communities: Improving outcomes in urban high schools.* New York, NY: Teachers College Press.

Wilson, W. J. (2009). The political and economic forces shaping concentrated poverty. *Political Science Quarterly, 123*(4), 555–571.

Youdell, D. (2003). Identity traps or how black students fail: The interactions between biographical, sub-cultural, and learner identities. *British Journal of Sociology of Education, 24*(1), 3–20.

Youdell, D. (2006). *Impossible bodies, impossible selves: Exclusion and student subjectivities.* Dordrecht: Springer.

2

MS. TURNER'S CLASSROOM: PRESERVING A TRADITION

The previous chapter focused on the role that Oxford High School, a symbol of the urban education tale, played on students' self-concepts and academic identity. This chapter takes an intimate look at the classroom in which participants experienced honors precalculus. Learning experiences that not only reinforced their beliefs in the existence of a math person but that also informed part of their postsecondary decisions.

This section of the book pays close attention to Ms. Turner. She was participants' mathematics teacher for half or most of their secondary education. Moreover, she knew many of the students very well. So, in my view, it was impossible, and likely a mistake, to separate her views of mathematics education, her assumptions about the idea of a math person, from the classroom culture in which participants continued to cultivate their relationship to mathematics. Her many decades teaching mathematics in underresourced, racially, and socioeconomically segregated public schools provide both context and a way to explore the combination of disparaging views of urban public schools and existing race-based beliefs that pervade mathematics education.

MS. TURNER

This book would not be possible without the generosity and overall support of Ms. Turner, the lead teacher of the honors precalculus class. She made herself and classroom available to me immediately and throughout this project. She never seemed bothered by my presence. Ms. Turner, a white woman in her 60s, shared her thoughts and lived experiences with me freely and regularly.

I was even privy to aspects of her life that had nothing to do with teaching. For instance, she revealed, during one of our many impromptu meetings, that her ex-husband's struggles with substance abuse derailed her plans for motherhood – this was in response to my opening up about the haunting and chilling effects that my nonexistent relationship with my father had on my prospects of having kids.

Students, including this study's participants, were incredibly comfortable confiding in Ms. Turner, and in some instances, grateful for having her as their teacher. This was evidenced in the countless "nonacademic" interactions observed and documented for this study. Those conversations took place mostly during Ms. Turner's lunch or prep periods. They were often in hushed tone, away from others' gazes, and out of earshot. Those moments crystalized the deeply compassionate and genuine relationships that she had cultivated with a number of students, some of whom not even enrolled in any of her math classes, but many dealing with very trying home lives.

> Elena, a junior enrolled in the college pipeline program, just came back from a 2–3-week hiatus. She had to find a shelter for her and her siblings. Elana was often in Ms. Turner's room during lunch. According to Ms. Turner, she was the victim of sexual abuse. Elana and her siblings had to be removed from their home, away from her alleged abuser. Ms. Turner was the one who alerted the authorities (without warning anyone else at Oxford). This caused friction between Ms. Turner and an Oxford's counselor who was working with Elena. The school failed to properly document Elena's case; the counselor was slow devising an adequate action plan. Ms. Turner didn't care; she understood and performed her "mandated reporter" duty to the letter.

This chapter is not an evaluation of Ms. Turner as a teacher, nor is it an endorsement or indictment of a particular pedagogy. Public distrust of teachers has grown popular in the past few decades. It has become an integral part of the neoliberal and market-based campaign to undermine public education and deprofessionalize the teaching profession (Lipman, 2011). Overreliance on standardized test scores has unfairly blamed "bad" teaching for why children and schools "fail" (Meyer, 2013, p. 5). As Koretz (2008) warned:

> …[w]hen a school performs well or poorly on an achievement test, the reason can be the quality of education, any number of non-educational causes, or – more likely – both. Figuring out which is

the case is not always easy...People routinely misinterpret differences
in test scores, commonly attributing more to quality of education
than they ought.

(pp. 117–118)

School teachers, students, and their families have all been spotlighted as the reason for the unfulfilled promises of the American public education experiment. They each have shouldered the blame for the contradictions of upholding public schools' democratic ideals in a profit-driven economy. Only 11% of Oxford High School's students scored proficient or better in their algebra state tests during the 2015–16 academic year. Investigations into "why" would likely only concentrate on teaching effectiveness and instructional methods. Explanations would undoubtedly seek to reaffirm the urban education tale and reify the notion that Black and Brown teenagers and their communities are simply anti-education. There would be no mention or account of "decades of disinvestment in physical, economic, and social infrastructure in areas where African Americans and other people of color live" (Lipman, 2011, p. 47). Nor would there be any inquiries into the availability of antiracist educational initiatives or professional development opportunities for Oxford teachers; no investigations into the school district's immediate plans and vision for addressing the existence and persistence of racial inequality in mathematics education.

Indeed, what follows is not another argument, nor should it be viewed ammunition for the "de-professionalization" of the teaching profession. It is an illustration of the real casualties of continued government's disinvestment in urban school districts; it is a case study of the complexities and salience of race-based injustice and discrimination in mathematics education.

"IT'S THAT PERSONALITY"

Ms. Turner's math classroom experiences, as a student and an educator, the scant resources for professional development available at Oxford High School and in the district of Philadelphia, limited her view of what it means to teach and learn mathematics. A history of injustices perpetrated against urban cities, their communities, and neighborhood public schools, and the ensuing disparaging view of schools like Oxford as perennial failures have shaped Ms. Turner's identity and perceived social function as an educator.

Before Oxford, Ms. Turner worked at Audenried High School, a public school, in South Philadelphia, and prior to that, she taught at a small private catholic school. When asked to compare her experience in public and private schools, Ms. Turner explained that students in the private faith-based school "weren't the brightest kids in the world"; however,

> *...they did their homework, knew their math facts, and had families that did flashcards with them. You had a few that didn't but they stood out, they weren't the norm. At [Oxford] we don't have that. We have some; but, again there are the rare ones. In the honor's class, that's where I think most of those good, solid families are.*

This is a derivative of the urban education tale; a "prevailing [unsubstantiated] view of many that Black and Latin[x] parents are disinterested in students' education" (Walker, 2012, p. 30). In spite of her very close relationships with students, Ms. Turner never visited them at home. She was not close with any of the students' parents or families. However, she was convinced that Oxford's overall performance grade of 1 out of 10 was the result of too few students from "good, solid families." She viewed the majority of Oxford students' sociocultural backgrounds as "obstacles" to their academic growth; she perceived them and their communities to be "innately disadvantaged" (Ladson-Billings, 2017, p. 81).

There is an urgent need for more dissemination and greater awareness of studies that do document the rich history and legacy of academic achievement promoted and fostered in underresourced communities of color (Walker, 2012, pp. 29–30; see also Anderson, 1988; Perry, Steele, & Hilliard, 2003; Siddle-Walker, 1996). Otherwise, this idea of urban communities and their school-aged children as "antiintellectual" and culturally inferior will not only persist but also continue to shape well-intentioned educators' view of Black and Brown students. This urban education tale about "who" and "what" it means to be a student at Oxford or to grow up in the surrounding community will continue to limit understanding of many students' true academic potential and relationships to schooling.

During her interview, when prompted to name students in her honors Algebra II and precalculus whom she considered "math people," Ms. Turner named three students of Vietnamese background:

> *I know that I'm picking my Asian students who people will automatically think it's because of [their race]. But no, it's their personality. They're calm. They don't always get it right away but they're patient. They would sit and they would listen; they just like calm themselves down. They're learning. It is that personality.*

Decades of teaching in underresourced, and racially and socioeconomically segregated public schools erected in her consciousness a fixed conception and image of what and who is a math person. Even though she considered the students observed for this book to be from "good, solid families," she could not envision them as belonging to the exclusive community of doers of mathematics. She couldn't see this study's participants as math people. They lack "that personality"; they did not fit the image of the "talented [Asian or White] mathematics student – [a] quiet, [and] quick completer of exercises" (Walker, 2012, p. 112).

Romeo and Stewart (1999) defined a "master narrative" as "familiar... inevitable and obvious stories we were taught and teach ourselves about who does what and why" (p. XIV). For instance, Andrew Yang, former 2020 contender for the Democratic Party's nomination, repeated throughout his campaign and live debates, without much backlash or resistance from mainstream American and international media, that being "Asian" meant that he was "good at math," thus, best suited to solve America's problems – never mind that he majored in political science in college, was a corporate lawyer later in life, and more recently is the founder of a successful nonprofit organization (Wikipedia Contributors, 2020, para. 6–17). Mr. Yang did not need to justify or substantiate his claim; no one needed an explanation for why he identified as a "math person." Master narratives are rarely questioned or challenged; "they gain strength from repetition and mirroring...and [by] erasing plot elements that don't fit" (Romeo & Stewart, 1999, p. XIV). For Ms. Turner, labeling a group of Black students, from Oxford High School, math people were "plot elements" that did not fit the urban education tale; it was a narrative that could not fit her beliefs about "what" and "who" is a math person.

Mathematics teachers, when prompted, are more likely than other educators to claim "racial differences" insignificant and unrelated to the math classroom (Gay, 2002; Ladson-Billings, 2009). The belief among them is that integrating the study of racial inequality and other social injustices in math curricula and instructions will cause "too much of a conceptual and substantive stretch...to maintain disciplinary integrity" (Gay, 2002, p. 107). Well-intentioned, competent, and seasoned mathematics teachers, like Ms. Turner, knowingly or unwittingly, find themselves in the role of defending and upholding a tradition rooted in racist ideology.

This is a consequence of a history of marginalizing racial equity in public debates and mainstream initiatives on how to innovate mathematics education (Berry, Pinter, & McClain, 2013; Gutstein, 2003; Martin, 2003). This legacy has persisted and continues to manifest itself in teacher training programs across the United States which focus, mostly or exclusively, on "classical" mathematics (Gutstein, 2003). Thus, pervasive beliefs of who is predisposed to succeed or fail in mathematics, this supposedly universal and value-free body of knowledge, are not only unaddressed but also allowed space to seep into teacher's perception of students, mold expectations, and shape learning environments.

CLASSROOM CULTURE

The honors precalculus class was not different from many other math classrooms that I have been in as a teacher or a student. Most of the time, students sat in individual desks arranged in rows and were facing an interactive white board (Smartboard); the latter's wide base and seven-foot height swallowed a big chunk of the front of the classroom. Lessons followed a mostly teacher-centered and skills-focused approach. Ms. Turner or a student teacher controlled and dictated most aspects of the learning. In some respects, the honors math class represented an illustration of the stubbornness of teacher-centered pedagogies in American education, especially math classrooms.

Some of the lessons or mathematical tasks designed for the honors precalculus class were based on Star's (2005) concept of "deep procedural knowledge" which he described as "knowledge of procedures associated with comprehension, flexibility, and critical judgment" (p. 408). This was part of the pedagogical orientation of the college pipeline program, which aimed at creating more opportunities for exploratory learning, and more emphasis on conceptual understanding and critical thinking. For students in the college pipeline program, this meant shifting away from instructional practices focused on getting the right answer or using the right procedure. More classroom time was supposed to be devoted on deepening mathematical understanding, flexible problem-solving ability, and analytical competencies. The data collected from my observation of Ms. Turner's math class told a different story.

Ms. Turner had been teaching mathematics for over 30 years and experienced a mostly teacher-centered and skills-focused mathematics education as a student. She conceded during her interview that she wished that current trends in math education would reconsider the value of "rote learning":

> ...when I was younger we did a lot of rote learning. We had to memorize our math facts, memorize our square roots, memorize our perfect squares. I think they need to bring that back because I think that there's a benefit to rote learning. I don't think it should be

> *utilized all the time but I think there're certain basic things that*
> *should be learned in that manner.*

This is getting at the heart of the "math wars" from the 1990s and the ongoing contentious debate over the pedagogical merit of skills-based/direct instructions versus more process-oriented or student-centered approaches to teaching (Klein, 2003; Schoenfeld, 2004). Ms. Turner echoed scholars' concerns, from various fields, that positioning skills-based teaching against fostering conceptual understanding was flawed and likely to be a disservice to many students (e.g. Delpit, 1988; Goldblatt, 1995; Star, 2005). She cautioned against teaching based exclusively on a "drill-and-kill" approach, or solely for the purpose of facilitating memorization of facts.

Most of the students in the honors precalculus class responded positively to Ms. Turner's teaching methods. During their interviews, many described her as one of the "best math teacher" they have had in their K–12 education:

> *...when [we] have a question for her, she just looked at it and had a*
> *vision of what she had to do to get the right answer every time.*

Because of this, a few participants thought that it was insulting and unfair for teaching assistants Mr. Bond or Mr. London – prospective teachers in training at Cecil B. Moore's college of education program – to teach whole lessons for many consecutive days. In Nigel's view, student teachers should not be "experimenting" on him; they should not be "learning how to teach" at his expense while a veteran educator was standing nearby. There were many moments recorded in my field notes where students resisted or complained about having to explore the meaning behind a particular mathematical rule. One common grievance, shared by some students, was that the college pipeline's emphasis on comprehension and flexibility in problem-solving was "making things difficult for no reason." Other students, over time, grew more intolerant of the student teachers' occasional faux pas or lack of clarity in the presentation of a concept or the description of a task. In contrast, throughout this study, whether during informal conversations or from their interviews' transcripts, participants consistently expressed genuine respect and appreciation for Ms. Turner as a mathematics teacher. There were no instances of students leveling criticisms against her teaching style or its effectiveness.

Students' perception and expectation of mathematics education as teacher-dominated and skills-based is explained in Martin's (2000) study of middle-school boys in a nontraditional algebra course. The author focused on a group of Black boys enrolled in a course that sought to "make connections between real-world events" in students' lives and "formal mathematics of algebra" (p. 104). Martin found that the majority of students observed in his study demonstrated very little interest in this "new" way of doing mathematics. Having experienced "traditional" mathematics for most of their schooling, they had "developed certain expectations" for what it meant to do mathematics (p. 178).

Similarly, students, observed for this book, accumulated experiences in K–12 mathematics classrooms that conflicted with the college pipeline's emphasis on "flexibility" in problem-solving. This study's participants and Ms. Turner shared a perception of mathematics education and a relationship to the discipline that, when challenged or questioned, resulted into resistance, protests, and congenial feelings about the need to protect a tradition. Both teacher and students felt compelled to preserve the "identity" of what they have been trained to accept and expect as mathematics teaching and learning.

PRESERVING A TRADITION OF EXCLUSION

Ms. Turner seemed unwilling to give serious consideration to pedagogies and methods of instruction different from the ones that she spent more than 30 years developing, refining, and testing in classrooms across the district of Philadelphia. A team of Cecil B. Moore's doctoral students and faculty members created the lessons for the college pipeline program – this was discussed and agreed upon during the summer months preceding the 2015–16 academic year. Lessons were sent to Oxford's teachers participating in the program via electronic mail. It was routine to observe her scheme through a lesson minutes and sometimes seconds before students began trickling into the room. Ms. Turner and I never discussed her seeming reluctance to review the lessons and plan their implementations. I never felt comfortable bringing it up. The closest we came to a conversation about how she prepared for the honors precalculus class was during her interview. Even then, I was careful to frame my question more as an inquiry into her philosophy of education and her beliefs about teaching mathematics:

> *I'll do my lessons [for the other two math classes] in the morning because those are the ones that I prepared for myself. I'll always look to see because I know the topics we're supposed to be teaching. They give us the book and you're free to teach anything in the book. There's about 7 key things that I always like try to get them to understand.*

Her teaching philosophy anchored on decades of experiential knowledge. She discovered, at some point during her career, the "key things" or ingredients necessary for a successful math classroom. She figured how to simplify instructional strategies and adopt tools to ease the all too familiar distaste that students, by secondary school, harbor for mathematics. Ms. Turner had a very warm, approachable, and self-deprecating classroom persona that helped to foster a "low-anxiety [learning] environment" (Young, 1991). This was her way of encouraging or making it easier for more students to engage with the more abstract mathematical concepts in precalculus.

Her noncommittal attitude toward the college pipeline program, in my view, should be framed as an unwitting refusal or resistance to subject over 30 years of professional experience and expertise to any kind of scrutiny or change. Perhaps, Ms. Turner, in spite of joining the program willingly, viewed the college pipeline program's takeover of the honors precalculus curricula and lesson planning as part of a larger political and economic shift in the United States to scapegoat, delegitimize, and deprofessionalize the teaching profession (Lipman, 2011).

Three decades in poorly funded public schools have taught and trained Ms. Turner not only to understand her disciplinary obligations as a mathematics teacher but also to balance them against her perceived social function as an educator responsible for a classroom of mostly kids from communities trapped in concentrated multigenerational poverty (Sharkey, 2013). During her interview, she explained that her

> ...job as math teachers is to make students function in the world they're living in. And [that] solving quadratic equations is not gonna come up that often in their real world.

Ms. Turner was attuned to the extracurricular challenges that some of her students experienced daily. She was also aware that kids from low-income communities, like this study's participants, often exhibit greater difficulty "setting their reality aside to engage in mathematics classroom investigations that do not connect to their reality" (McNair, 2000, p. 559; see also Bruckerhoff, 1995). In her view, her role as an educator was divided between attending to students' lives outside of the classroom and teaching them the "key things" necessary to be proficient in secondary mathematics.

Ms. Turner viewed students' *lifeworlds* and academic needs as separate and competing forces. She believed that the more advanced and abstract aspects of mathematics (e.g. solving quadratic equations) had no utility for most Oxford students. In the excerpt cited above, Ms. Turner echoed early 1900s progressive views and warning about mathematics' "harmful rather than helpful" effects on "the kind of thinking necessary for ordinary living" (Klein, 2003, p. 178). However, the twenty-first century's global economy is becoming increasingly more dependent on technology, a scientifically and mathematically competent workforce. Therefore, as was observed by Moses and Cobb (2001), access to quality mathematics education has become the new millennium's civil rights issue; it's the "most urgent social issue affecting poor people and people of color" (p. 5).

The economic or social mobility argument for making quality mathematics education accessible to students from communities devastated by and still enduring this country's history of racist policies is complex. For one, as discussed later in this book, reforms in the field of mathematics tend to subscribe to neoliberal and market-based ideologies that favor competition and presume an equal playing field (Gutstein, 2009). Second, those initiatives tend to be motivated by a fear or anxiety around America's slipping world dominance (pp. 137–139). Black and Brown students, like the students enrolled at Oxford High School, are rarely viewed, taught, and supported as the "talents" or future high-skilled workers needed to "salvage" the country's "economic supremacy" (p. 138). So, while it's undeniable that mathematics is a gatekeeper to economic opportunities and participation into very lucrative sectors of the American labor market, traditional views about what it means to teach mathematics and who can be math people need to change drastically before math classrooms can truly be considered a viable path out of poverty for some Black Americans and other communities of color.

This is a vivid illustration of what I considered to be one of the more serious missteps of a century-long fight to reform mathematics without addressing the discipline's race-based exclusionary history. Ms. Turner's undeniable passion for teaching and dedication to the welfare and success of her students were obfuscated by her narrow conception of mathematics education, a superficial and distorted interpretation of decades of working in underfunded segregated public school districts. Nothing in her training as a preservice teacher, in-service professional development requirements, or in mainstream mathematics education reform initiatives (e.g. National Council of Teachers of Mathematics (NCTM's) *Mathematics for All*) provided her the opportunity and experience necessary to envision math classrooms as sites wherein it is possible to foster students' "sociopolitical consciousness...sense of social agency...and positive social/cultural identities" (Gutstein, 2006, p. 332). Instead, Ms. Turner, like many other seasoned, caring, and competent urban public school teachers, found herself in the untenable position of having to choose between students' academic needs and helping them navigate the crippling, lasting impact of de jure socioeconomic and racial segregation of several decades ago.

CONCLUSION

Protecting the "identity" of what is mathematics shaped much of the context in which this study's participants experienced precalculus, and presumably, most of their secondary education.

Ms. Turner's class was not atypical of the traditional and still predominant conception of a mathematics classroom fashioned after the "transmission model" – students' role is primarily that of a "knowledge consumer" at the mercy of the teacher, the sole "knowledge producer" (McNair, 2000, p. 551). As stated earlier, my intention in this section was not to evaluate Ms. Turner's teaching methods; nor was it to comment on the merit of skills-based pedagogies compared to process-oriented teaching. However, learning experiences that do not encourage or allow space to envision mathematics education beyond a classroom's walls, outside of a history of exclusion, and as a challenge to a tradition rooted in racist ideology will continue to alienate the same groups of students.

The next two chapters will focus on how classroom experiences and narratives about what and who is math person molded and limited students' relationship to mathematics.

REFERENCES

Anderson, J. D. (1988). *The education of Blacks in the South 1860–1935*. Chapel Hill, NC: University of North Carolina Press.

Berry, R. Q., Pinter, H. H., & McClain, O. L. (2013). A critical review of K-12 mathematics education, 1900-present. In J. Leonard & D. B. Martin (Eds.), *The brilliance of Black children in mathematics: Beyond the numbers and toward new discourse* (pp. 23–53). Charlotte, NC: Information Age Publishing.

Bruckerhoff, C. (1995). Life in the bricks. *Urban Education, 30*(3), 317–336.

Delpit, L. (1988). The silenced dialogue: Power and pedagogy in educating other people's children. *Harvard Educational Review, 58*(3), 280–298.

Gay, G. (2002). Preparing for culturally responsive teaching. *Journal of Teacher Education, 53*(2), 106–116.

Goldblatt, E. C. (1995). *'Round my way: Authority and double-consciousness in three urban high school writers*. Pittsburgh, PA: University of Pittsburgh Press.

Gutstein, E. (2003). Teaching and learning mathematics for social justice in an urban, Latino school. *Journal for Research in Mathematics Education, 34*(1), 37–73.

Gutstein, E. (2006). "The real world as we have seen it": Latino/a parents voice on teaching mathematics for social justice. *Mathematical Thinking and Learning, 8*(3), 331–358.

Gutstein, E. (2009). The politics of mathematics education in the US: Dominant and counter agendas. In B. Greer, S. Mukhopadhyay, A. B. Powell, & S. Nelson-Barber (Eds.), *Culturally responsive mathematics education* (pp. 137–164). New York, NY: Routledge.

Klein, D. (2003). A brief history of American K-12 mathematics education in the 20th century. In J. M. Royer (Ed.), *Mathematical cognition* (pp. 175–225). Greenwich, CT: Information Age Publishing.

Koretz, D. (2008). *Measuring up: What educational testing really tells us.* Cambridge, MA: Harvard University Press.

Ladson-Billings, G. (2009). *The dream-keepers: Successful teachers of African American children.* San Francisco, CA: Jossey-Bass.

Ladson-Billings, G. (2017). "Makes me wanna holler": Refuting the "culture of poverty" discourse in urban schooling. *The Annals of the American Academy of Political and Social Science, 673*(1), 80–90. doi:10.1177/0002716217718793

Lipman, P. (2011). *The new political economy of urban education: Neoliberalism, race, and the right to the city.* New York, NY: Taylor & Francis.

Martin, D. B. (2000). *Mathematics success and failure among African-American youth: The roles of sociohistorical context, community forces, school influence, and individual agency.* New York, NY: Routledge.

Martin, D. B. (2003). Hidden assumptions and unaddressed questions in *Mathematics for all* in rhetoric. *The Mathematics Educator, 13*(2), 7–21.

McNair, R. E. (2000). Life outside of mathematics classroom: Implications for mathematics reform. *Urban Education, 34*(5), 550–570.

Meyer, R. J. (2013). The truth behind manufactured malpractice: The impact of NCLB upon literacy teaching and learning. *New England Reading Association, 49*(1), 1–6.

Moses, R. P., & Cobb, C. E. (2001). *Radical equations: Civil rights from Mississippi to the Algebra Project*. Boston, MA: Beacon Press.

Perry, T., Steele, C., & Hilliard, A. G. (2003). *Young, gifted, and Black: Promoting high achievement among African-American students*. Boston, MA: Beacon Press.

Romeo, M., & Stewart, A. J. (Eds.). (1999), *Women's untold stories: Breaking silence, talking back, voicing complexity*. New York, NY: Routledge.

Schoenfeld, A. H. (2004). The math wars. *Educational Policy, 18*, 253–286.

Sharkey, P. (2013). *Stuck in place: Urban neighborhoods and the end of progress to ward racial equality*. Chicago, IL: The University of Chicago Press.

Siddle-Walker, V. (1996). *Their highest potential: An African American school community in the segregated South*. Chapel Hill, NC: University of North Carolina Press.

Star, J. R. (2005). Reconceptualizing procedural knowledge. *Journal for Research in Mathematics Education, 36*(5), 404–411.

Walker, E. N. (2012). *Building mathematics learning communities: Improving outcomes in urban high schools*. New York, NY: Teachers College Press.

Wikipedia Contributors. (2020, August 24). Andrew Yang. In *Wikipedia, the free encyclopedia*. Retrieved 14:50 from https://en.wikipedia.org/w/index.php?title=Andrew_Yang&oldid=974766428. Accessed on August 26, 2020.

Young, D. J. (1991). Creating a low-anxiety classroom environment: What language anxiety research suggest? *The Modern Language Journal, 75*(4), 426–439.

3

WHAT IS A MATH PERSON?

The previous chapter looked at the classroom culture in which participants experienced honors precalculus. This chapter examines key patterns that emerged out of a multilevel analysis of students' accumulated experiences in mathematics classrooms and how those experiences informed their conception of a math person and helped to shape the content of their math identities.

A "GREAT THINKER"

Students in Ms. Turner's honors precalculus class were, like most Americans, conditioned to believe and expect that "only a select few people" can and will succeed in math (Walker, 2012, p. 8). They viewed a math person as someone whose success in the classroom is predetermined and preconditioned at birth. To them, math people's success, the manifestation of a biological fact, is independent of pedagogy, teacher effectiveness, and is impervious to extra-curricular forces.

Shalik was one of the highest performing students in Ms. Turner's class and one of the most consistently engaged. However, when presented with a math problem, his instinct was to blurt out "I don't know how to do this" – this became our inside joke. After guiding him a little bit or reminding him of a concept, he was usually among the first students to complete the task in question. He volunteered, happily and often, to share his work with the whole class or just classmates near him. Shalik was an aspiring dancer. He and Stephanie were enrolled in dance classes and competed in local contests. Ms. Turner showed me a video of the two competing in a dance contest – it is worth noting that she was very eager to show me the clip and so visibly proud of them. Shalik's relationship to mathematics was a bit enigmatic.

However, his belief in the existence of a math person and his understanding of what it means to be such a person were very commonplace. During his first interview, Shalik observed that someone who can

> ...figure out a problem no matter if it is with radicals, variables, just numbers, or complex numbers, and is able to break it down to get the answer every time, without help, is a math person.

Stephanie, one of Shalik's closest friends, felt similarly. But, she added another dimension to the idea of math person. Stephanie never considered herself "good" at math – this is in spite of a history of mostly successes in mathematics. Math people, in her eyes, are born with an uncanny ability to remember a "bunch of rules" and know when to apply them. Something she could not do; a trait and an aptitude that she was certain most people did not possess. Mathematics, from Stephanie's perspective, "is one of those subjects where it's either you like it and you know it, or you hate it and you don't."

Kendrick, the only participant born outside of the United States, had experiences and demonstrated levels of engagement that diametrically opposed Shalik's and others in honors precalculus. He was usually quiet in class. Kendrick never volunteered to solve a problem or answer a question. In fact, there's no record of him asking a question aloud – he did call me, the student teacher, or Ms. Turner to his desk occasionally. Kendrick added that a math person "is a great thinker" because they:

> ...know and use everything [they] were taught. They can look at a problem, be smart [about it] and think about everything to get the answer.

Nigel echoed him. He argued that if you're a math person, you already "know it as child if you're good with numbers or not." He conceded that math people don't "really [need] to study" to do well. He was an "A student" until his 12th and final year of secondary education. He felt like he never "really" studied to succeed in math classrooms; he was born "good with numbers." Nigel, who considered himself a math person during the course of this study, did not see the point of "trying hard" in 12th grade, especially in a math course that wasn't a requirement for graduation. He explained that he was tired; senior year was time to finally "rest because of all the stuff [he's] been pressured over like all these years, all these extra stuff." He also refused to entertain the possibility of pursuing a science, technology, engineering, and mathematics (STEM) major or career because of the anticipated "hassle" of dealing with advanced math in college.

Victor, like Kendrick, struggled to keep up with the honors precalculus curriculum. He was also intent on avoiding advanced college math. He characterized higher lever math as only useful to a selected few who, like "astronauts," were capable of engaging with content inaccessible to most people within planet earth's orbit.

Other participants and other students in Ms. Turner's class also believed in the existence of a math person. Their definition mirrored, almost identically, what Shalik, Stephanie, Kendrick, Nigel, and Victor said above. Most in the honors precalculus class subscribed to the notion of the mythical math person: someone born with otherworldly capacity for abstract thinking and sophisticated computations.

The idea of "struggle" did not feature in students' conception and explanation of what it means to be a math person. In fact for many, not understanding a concept or not knowing the "right" procedure to solving a mathematical task meant that you lacked the "superpowers" needed to be a doer of mathematics. As Kendrick observed, math people can "look at a problem and be smart about it"; they figure out the correct approach immediately.

> There is a prevalent view that people who do well in mathematics do so "naturally." Consequently, unlike other disciplines that we believe require hard work – good writing can be developed, for example – our societal emphasis [is] on mathematics as a difficult subject in which we expect a few people do well.
>
> (Walker, 2012, p. 8)

Unlike other disciplines, like history, or literature, where expertise in a specific branch or area of focus (e.g. "I am a postmodernist scholar") and unfamiliarity with other aspects of the discipline is the norm, the requisite for a math person, at least from students' perspective and classroom experiences, seems to be facility for all of mathematics' major divisions. This was a common thread in participants' individual stories about mathematics education. As Shalik pointed out, a math person is expected "to break down" any problem without assistance. Math people distinguish themselves from everyone else precisely because they represent a very small and exclusive group of "great thinkers" who can meet the impossible cognitive demands of remembering and applying a "bunch of rules."

This belief is crystalized in secondary education where students engage with increasingly more theoretical mathematics often taught in ways that force them to bracket off their instincts, interests, and worldviews. High school math requires students to draw a rather rigid and seemingly impenetrable line between mathematical knowledge and almost everything else that they've learned, might be interested in learning, or are aspired to be. By their 12th year of mathematics education, the students in Ms. Turner's class had been socialized to ascribe the label "math people" to rare breeds, with extraterrestrial talents, and who are predisposed to solve any problem, including the ones based on content that "[they] haven't been taught" yet.

Recent reform initiatives aimed at connecting mathematical content to students' social realities have received a fair amount of criticisms and resistance from members of the mathematics community (e.g. Harel & Koichu, 2010). Critics of mathematics education's recent shifts have expressed concerns over the growing number of scholarship "unrelated" to or not focused enough on "classical" mathematics. Those critics, as Aguirre et al. (2017) observed, tend to respond to studies like this book with questions such as: "Where is the mathematics in this scholarship?" or "What percentage of work is mathematics and what percentage is equity?" (pp. 130–131). Efforts to move the field of mathematics education beyond its assumed neutrality and presumed universal standards have been characterized as a threat to the discipline's integrity and "identity."

NTCM's (2010) sponsored symposium entitled *Keeping the Mathematics in Mathematics Education Research* is an illustration of the resistance that studies like this book have received. The symposium reasserted the prevailing wisdom that mathematical knowledge is defined and should be restricted to "all ways of understanding and...thinking that have been institutionalized throughout history" (Harel & Koichu, 2010, p. 116; see Harel, 2008). Harel (2008) explained that creativity in mathematics is "mathematical" only if it is consistent with existing "institutionalized" mathematical knowledge, or is accepted by the "existing edifice of mathematics" (p. 10). I do not have any objections to the aforementioned. Nor is this book or the budding movement that made it possible advocating for the abolition of the "existing edifice of mathematics."

However, calls and pressure to "keep the mathematics in mathematics education" can, and will likely, shore up beliefs of the existence of a math person. The discrediting, delegitimizing, and marginalizing of scholarships that seek to unearth mathematics' racist, sexist, and elitist history is the surest way to uphold, normalize, and continue a tradition premised on "limiting meaningful participation in schools and society" for groups historically underrepresented in STEM fields (Martin, 2003, p. 17).

Challenging the legacy of a field that prides itself on exclusivity (i.e. inequality) is not an attack on the integrity or identity of mathematics education. It is a reckoning – an evaluation and judgment – guided by one of the most fundamental principles of a social justice education: "education as the practice of freedom...that considers...people in their relations with the world" (Freire, 1970, p. 81).

TAMIKA AND STEPHANIE: A "BUNCH OF RULES"

The honors students who participated in this study cultivated a perception of mathematics consistent with the central themes of NTCM's (2010) *Keeping the Mathematics in Mathematics Education Research*. This perception of mathematics constrained their relationships to the discipline and complicated their interpretations of success in math classrooms. By senior year, mathematics represented a threat and potential barrier to most participants' academic and professional aspirations (Table 3.1).

Table 3.1. Profile of Participants' Math Experience and Identity.

Participants	Interpretation of Overall Experience	Math Identity (during Study)
Kawhi Weldon	Mostly positive; Math was their most "comfortable" subject; Saw themselves as "numbers" people.	Math people
Shalik	Mostly positive; Did well in K–12 math; Lost confidence in high school.	No longer a math person
Tamika Stephanie	Worked hard; Earned good grades; Saw K–12 math as a "struggle."	Never were math people
Tyronne Victor	Positive until high school; Were treated as "example"; Math students in earlier grades; Higher math is for "astronauts";	Math people
Kendrick	Positive until high school; Was "pretty fast with that stuff"; Never considered a math career;	No longer a math person
Nigel Andre Felix	Mostly positive; Always enjoyed math; Believed to be "numbers" people; College math will be a "hassle."	Math people

This was especially true for Tamika and Stephanie, the hardest working and among the highest achieving students interviewed and observed for this book.

Tamika was another participant who performed very well in honors precalculus. She believed that she was not a math person because she was "too creative with [her] thoughts." She wanted to major in psychology or another field that allows to use her talents and interests in people. Mathematics, in her view, does not offer opportunities for creativity, nor is it interested in students' instincts or curiosities. She could not envision mastering all of the "institutionalized ways of understanding" that define mathematics. This was particularly hard because she was never taught to use her "creative thoughts" to learn or make sense of mathematics. Tamika acknowledged that she was among the highest performing students in the honors precalculus class but said that it had nothing to do with mathematical ability or academic potential.

> *Researcher: Any time between Kindergarten and now, even for a quarter, or a month, a week that you felt like maybe I'm a math person?*
>
> *Tamika: No. No.*
>
> *Researcher: Never?*
>
> *Tamika: Never*
>
> *Researcher: Even when you got 100% on a test?*
>
> *Tamika: No, I just think that I studied as hard as I could and I got a good grade.*

Success in math classrooms did not translate into academic confidence. Tamika conceded that "hard work" could or, in her case, did result in good grades. She had a working formula – one with a history of success. However, as it pertained to her postsecondary education, deciding between fostering her creative capacities and studying "as hard as she could" to enter or survive a field reserved for "geniuses" was not much of a choice.

Stephanie, like Tamika, was one of the most studious students in the class. She was often on task and worked earnestly to complete her independent practice problems. Stephanie and I got along almost immediately. We both shared a history with and interests in the performing arts. Many of our side conversations revolved around figuring out a balance between pursuing her passions for the arts and obeying her parents' wishes – choosing a "practical" college major. Stephanie was not shy about asking for help; nor was she ever afraid to question or challenge mathematical concepts or procedures that seemed to defy logic. She was certain that she was not a math person. Her successes in honors precalculus and in previous math classes bore no significance; mathematics, to her, is a "bunch of rules" that she never "understood" and could never understand. Stephanie was accepted to a number of predominantly white institutions (PWIs) across Pennsylvania. Her motivation to do well academically stemmed from a perceived social responsibility that she, as a Black student, had to "prove them wrong." However, when it came to pursuing a math-focused college major, she viewed it as a "personal choice." Likewise, she was not interested in a PWI or the idea of being among mostly white students. She was weary of the anticipated "stress" of having to continually engage in *stereotype management* – figuring out ways to succeed or at least persevere "in the face of stereotypes" (McGee, 2013, p. 254).

Stephanie and Tamika were among a handful of students considered by their classmates and Ms. Turner to be very strong academically. A fact that was substantiated countless times during the course of this study. Nonetheless, they never felt competent enough to identify as math people. They summed up their experiences in math classrooms as a "struggle." In fact, both students did not have much confidence in their academic potential or prospects. Tamika routinely complained about her lack of academic preparedness and how her "inadequate" Oxford education would hinder her transition into college and professional life. Stephanie feared the Sisyphean task of disproving disparaging views of African Americans in college and among students of "other races" who typically behaved in ways that suggested that they knew more or were "smarter."

> *I don't want to be like one of those typical kids that drop out of college. They put so much work to get there and then they're like "oh, I can't do this." Or they don't wanna work. Again that goes with the simple issue of...stereotype, being that I'm African American [who] just graduated from high school.*

None of the successes that Stephanie and Tamika experienced in their K–12 classrooms proved sufficient to convince them that they were "great thinkers," nor did the many accolades that they received from peers and teachers. None of it was resonant or meaningful enough to dare take on the "impossible" disciplinary demands of being a "doer of mathematics." Stephanie and Tamika could not internalize their history of classroom successes at Oxford High School. They knew that their scholastic achievements, beyond Oxford, would be evaluated with suspicion and skepticism. The kind of suspicion or skepticism that I presume, in the wake of universities and colleges going Scholastic Aptitude Test (SAT)/American College Test (ACT) optional, will become a more integral part of the evaluation process of high-performing students from "low-performing," racially, and socioeconomically segregated urban schools.

> ...although grading standards do vary by school, [grade point averages] still outperform standardized tests [like the SATs] in predicting college outcomes: Irrespective of the quality or type of school attended, cumulative grade point average (GPA) in academic subjects in high school has proved to be the best overall predictor of student performance in college.
>
> (Atkinson & Geiser, 2009, p. 665)

This is another instance of the perniciousness of the urban education tale; as Shalik said, Oxford High School was not a "special admission school." Tamika and Stephanie were skeptical of the transferability of their academic experiences and achievements in the world outside of Oxford. They learned to be suspicious of the value of their academic history and potential, especially among people who were not part of their community.

The impact of rigid notions of a math person as someone born with math genes is particularly intriguing when considering the fact that Tamika and Stephanie, the only female participants in this study, summarized their entire K–12 mathematics education as a "struggle." Gender-based differences in mathematics is beyond the scope of this book, and neither of the participants pointed explicitly to their gender as an explanation for why they never identified with the discipline. Nonetheless, two high-performing female students incapable to see themselves as math people warrant further investigation and considerations of the pervasiveness of the "perception of mathematics as a content area more exclusive to males" (Harkness & Stallworth, 2013, p. 330).

Moreover, there is a dearth of scholarship and very limited knowledge about Black girls and women in the field of mathematics education. Gholson (2016) argued that mainstream:

> ...discourses of girls' "hyper achievement" and Black boys and men's "endangerment" produce an apathetic orientation to Black girls and women in mathematics education.
>
> (p. 292)

Tamika and Stephanie's stories are often left out of the extant literature. They are not only invisible, but their experiences and perspectives are deemed unimportant or unrelated to the fight against racial inequality in mathematics education.

The position of Black girls and women is typically invoked in mathematics to serve as referent in making sense of the conditions of other demographic groups, such as Black boys and White girls...Black girls and women do occasionally gain fleeting recognition in mathematics, but...after highlighting the conditions of other learners.

(p. 293; see Dotson & Gilbert, 2014)

This is further evidence of the urgent need for more studies to focus on mathematics identity development, with emphasis on the roles that gender – inclusive of genders that do not fit the traditional binary man–woman – and race, individually and collectively, play in students' perception of and relationship to mathematics education.

SHALIK, "I WAS BEFORE BUT I'M NOT ANYMORE"

Like Stephanie and Tamika, Shalik was a hardworking and an engaged student. His scores were also better than the class average. He volunteered frequently to solve and explain problems on the board. He offered suggestions and asked thoughtful questions regularly during class discussions. However, when prompted about enrolling in advanced college level math courses, his response was a categoric "no." Mathematics was not in his postsecondary plans. He no longer thought of himself as a math person:

Shalik: I felt like I was before but I'm not anymore.

Researcher: You wouldn't call yourself a math person now?

Shalik: No

Researcher: But, the 6th grade you, in 6th grade, if someone were to ask you, "are you a math person?" you would've said...

Shalik: Yeah.

Researcher: Why?

Shalik: Because I understood everything. You could throw me any math problem [at my grade level] and I would be able to answer it.

However, in honors precalculus, in spite of very good grades, despite actually "breaking down" many of the problems assigned to him, despite being the one helping classmates, Shalik could no longer imagine the label math person as a possibility. It was not befitting the academic or professional life he envisioned after high school. Similar to Stephanie and Tamika, he viewed a math person as someone wired to perform tasks that are inaccessible to most people, including himself.

The binary "math people" and "nonmath people" created a fascinating discordance in Shalik's experience with mathematics and interpretation of those experiences. During his first interview, I asked if he could identify a math person from a group of strangers:

> *Shalik: If I was to walk into a [math] classroom and didn't know anybody, the person who's the most engaged and the person who's willing to show what they're doing [is a math person]. Cause I know a lot of people are unsure when it comes to math.*
>
> *Researcher: Which means going to the board and do problems on the board, and helping others, right?*
>
> *Shalik: Yes.*
>
> *Researcher: These are all things that I watched you do. And you're still saying that you're not a math person?*
>
> *Shalik: I don't know. Maybe it's just because I know how to do it, [but] I just don't like it. So, I don't know.*

Shalik behaved exactly how he envisioned a math person would conduct themselves in a classroom – he was among "the most engaged," has helped others, and was always "willing to show what [he was] doing" on the board. Nonetheless, he refused to entertain the possibility that he may be one of the selected few geniuses. Instead, Shalik drew a distinction between engaging with advanced math, helping classmates and the archetypical math student, the ones expected to "populate" and succeed in the field of mathematics (Urrieta, 2007, p. 108). He amended his description of a math person just enough to justify why he did not and could not fit the label math person – "I know how to do it, [but] I just don't like it."

The trend of increased level of abstraction and sophistication in secondary mathematics education coupled with greater emphasis on teacher-centered pedagogy, rote learning, and traditional methods of assessments contribute to lower level of engagement for many high school students (Walker, 2012, pp. 74–75). In the case of Shalik, it distorted and limited his relationship to mathematics. High scores on tests or high level of engagement carried no significance or meaning. They could not compete against the pervasive view that success should come "easily" and "naturally" to math people.

In elementary and middle school where the use of hands-on activities are more prevalent and aspects of students' personal identity (e.g. racial identity) have yet to become a salient part of their self-concept (Tatum, 2017, p. 134), Shalik did consider himself a possible inheritor of those rare math genes. In secondary school, when the content got "harder," and "struggle" became a more regular part of the learning process, he and other participants reached the only conclusion available to them: we weren't born with the "math genes." Shalik was convinced that he could no longer meet the requisite criterion for a doer of mathematics – that is to solve every math problem "thrown" at him.

FROM "EXAMPLE KID" TO MATH PHOBIA

Unlike Stephanie, Tamika, and Shalik, some students in Ms. Turner's class struggled keeping pace with the academic rigor and exigencies of the college pipeline. For instance, Kendrick, Tyronne, and Victor were often lost or frustrated. The lesson was either going too fast or seemed too "complicated"; guided practice problems or tests were always too hard. Honors precalculus solidified their perception of mathematics as a gatekeeper or a "risk" too great for some students' postsecondary dreams.

Kendrick no longer identified as a math person during the course of this study. He blamed this on his first two years at Oxford:

> I missed some of the stuff; so, probably some of the stuff that I should be thinking about "like what to do" [to solve problem]. The way you need to look at a problem and be smart, maybe I'm not gonna be thinking [that way] cause I missed a little on my way. I missed some stuff.

Ms. Turner was absent for most of Kendrick's first year at Oxford High School. His second year was spent with another teacher who left the school within the first few months, presumably for a "better" opportunity. Kendrick believed that he was robbed of the education needed to "be smart" about the institutionalized ways of thinking about algebra. He remembered an entire academic year of a revolving door of substitute teachers, many of whom, in his eyes, unqualified or not certified to teach secondary mathematics.

Back in his native country of Jamaica, Kendrick's math experience and relationship to the discipline were markedly different.

> I was pretty fast with this stuff. Like [the teacher] could give me a problem that she didn't go over yet, like an advanced one and I

could look at it, and know what to do and get it right. Like me and
one of my friends, we used to get more advanced problems on the
board to do.

His experience in high school is unfortunately somewhat common. Many underresourced urban public schools in the US experience "shortages of high-quality teachers" perennially (Anyon, 1997; Liu, Rosenstein, Swan, & Khalil, 2008, p. 299). There is even a greater need for mathematics teachers in those districts. Schools like Oxford High School not only struggle staffing permanent teaching positions but also have a difficult time recruiting or retaining short- or long-term competent substitute teachers. The reasons why schools in cities like Philadelphia struggle attracting and retaining competent mathematics teachers range from inadequate funding, lower wages relative to neighboring suburban districts, and the fact that seasoned or qualified teachers tend to "migrate away from poor, low-performing 'minority' children" (p. 300; see also Hanushek, Kain, & Rivkin, 2001). Kendrick had a firsthand experience of teachers not wanting to teach or stay in low-income communities of color. An experience that not only contributed to a "gap" in his secondary mathematics education but also limited his vision and the assessment of his prospects after Oxford.

Kendrick was accepted to three four-year colleges but opted to enroll into a local community college. He wanted to major in Fire Science but was very anxious about having to take a mathematics college placement exam – students graduating high school with average or lower than average SAT or ACT scores are typically required to take college placement exams as part the admission process. Participants' SAT or ACT scores were not factored in this study for many reasons; most of which fall outside the purview of this book. However, it's important to underscore that standardized test scores do not offer much insight into how students developed their perception and relation to a discipline. Moreover, many "validity studies" have documented the predictive shortcomings and racial biases of aptitude tests like the SAT.

> *…mathematically-talented students in poor, predominantly Black*
> *environments might not have the same standardized test scores as*
> *higher achieving students from higher-income, higher-resourced*
> *schools due to the accumulation of inequities that Black students*
> *in under-resourced schools (neighborhoods, cities) endure and the*
> *bias of standardized testing itself, which favors White and higher*
> *income groups.*
>
> *(McGee, 2013, p. 256; see also Ford, 2011; Gutierrez, 2012)*

Biases that have served to reinforce or exacerbate existing race-based and other social inequalities. For Kendrick, and many other Black and Brown teenagers enrolled in schools like Oxford, aptitude tests or college placement exams are just part of the onslaught of never-ending reminders of their presumed academic and cultural inferiority.

Kendrick's decision to go to a community college was, in part, an attempt at avoiding college math. Kendrick's experiences in honors precalculus, his time at Oxford without a full-time, certified, and competent mathematics teacher made college math courses seem like an impossibility. By the time he sat down with me for an interview, being "pretty fast" in middle school was completely erased from the content of his math identity. An unshakable conviction about his "lack" of academic preparedness or potential had settled in; a rather paralyzing fear about life after high school was guiding most of Kendrick's plans.

Tyronne also pointed to institutional failures and larger social factors as reasons or explanations for the struggles and frustrations he endured in Ms. Turner's class. He hinted at "being caught up doing things outside of school" that derailed his initial academic trajectory. He was labeled an "example kid" in elementary school and received praises from his teachers, particularly in mathematics, regularly. During his first interview, Tyronne reflected on those moments:

> ...all the praise that my teachers were giving me for doing what I was supposed to do kinda threw me off. It's just like: "why ya'll acting like this?" I think back on it now, it's like "oh, we got this little black kid and he's doing his math"(laughter). I had good grasp on my math because my dad punished me with education. When I got in trouble in school, I would have to take a "Marble Notebook," like one of these (he was holding a notebook), and start from like my two times table up to my twelve and fill the book.

As a 17-year-old, those moments no longer carried the same meaning. In hindsight, those praises seemed odd and misplaced. They appeared unwarranted, and more like a manifestation or illustration of the idea of *learning mathematics while Black* – a set of "racialized constructions of who is considered mathematically literate and who is not" used in appraising, discussing, and thinking about Black students' mathematical aptitude (Martin, 2012, p. 50). Tyronne, the 12th grader about to transition into adulthood, reflecting on being an "example kid" is best understood in relationship to mathematics education's most enduring *master narratives* – African Americans are not mathematically inclined; Asian and white males are. The next chapter offers a deeper and more detailed account of how beliefs of a racial hierarchy of mathematics ability shaped this study's participants view of and relationship to math.

Tyronne's "example kid" status was interrupted abruptly. He was sent to an alternative Philadelphia public school. During our second interview, he summed up his two years at the alternative public school as "not really educational":

> I can't help but reflect on the days that I sat in my math class in middle school and did not do anything but watch the teacher break up fights.

Those years had an indelible impact on Tyronne's overall academic identity and relationship to mathematics. He, like most students in the honors precalculus class, had fulfilled his requirements for graduation months before the end of the 2015–16 academic year. He had the credentials to apply and likely be accepted into a number of colleges or universities in and surrounding the state of Pennsylvania. Nevertheless, as the prospect of becoming a college student looked more and more like reality, he started devising and implementing alternate plans. He decided to join the Navy full time.

Tyronne maintained that he was a math person during the course of this study. In fact, he probably never abandoned the label "example kid" acquired in elementary school. "I'm a pretty fast learner," he exclaimed, unprompted, early in his interview. The emphasis seemed to be a note to me and a reminder to himself that his performance in honors precalculus should not be considered a measure of his potential or motivation to succeed. However, those years spent at the alternative school, in his mind, put him too far behind, too far away from ever becoming fluent in all the ways of thinking and understanding college-level mathematics. Tyronne did not feel "college ready":

> ...one thing that really bugs me with most of this is that I keep telling myself that I can't go to [college] because the stuff that we're doing [in honor's pre-calculus] is like on entry exams everywhere and I'm just like then that means I can't come in because I don't, I don't get any of this... I always understood that there's definitely a way when there's a will and right now, I'm just preparing myself more or less.

The specter of college mathematics made it hard to imagine higher education as a viable pathway to professional and economic stability.

Similarly, Victor, another senior in this study whose overall experience in secondary mathematics classrooms was drastically different from his elementary and middle school years, drew a significant distinction between math people like himself who had no interest, felt no obligation to enroll in advanced college math courses, and others who were "willing to put in the time." Victor identified as a math person in spite of considerable struggles in high school math. However, by senior year, he viewed advanced math courses as a hard "game" unnecessary for his career path:

> I wouldn't wanna go spend years of my time [studying] math when I only wanna do this certain thing, this certain job. [Students who enrolled in advanced college math] probably decided they wanted to become accountants, make a lot of money...If I go to college to do advanced classes for math, it will be too hard for me and then when I do become a cop, I can't really do anything with the math.

Victor blamed some of his struggles in honors precalculus on having to work full time as a manager for a fast food restaurant near Oxford High School. He framed his disinterest in investing more time, effort, or money in higher level college math as an economic and commonsense decision. The frustrations he anticipated experiencing did not match the "modest" salary and job requirements of a police officer. Moreover, secondary mathematics education taught him that the math community was made up of individuals with a lot of time, singular cognitive capacities, and unusually high level of interest or tolerance for abstract thinking. None of it fitted Victor's life in high school; none of it appealed to him or made sense for the future he imagined.

Kendrick, Tyronne, and Victor represent illustrations of why many urban education scholars focus on the perniciousness of negative extracurricular and institutionalized forces on students' academic attainments. Even students labeled "great thinkers" during the early stage or midpoint of their K–12 education are not shielded or exempt from being pulled away from the academic path they began paving in elementary or middle school.

CONCLUSION

This chapter shows how participants' accumulated experiences in mathematics shaped their perceived math ability and potential. Seven of the 11 participants still identified as math people during the course of this study. However, their experiences in secondary education convinced most of them that college majors requiring advanced math courses is out of their reach or simply too much of a "hassle." This was true of Oxford's valedictorian who registered for a lower level college math course after being placed in Calculus I; it was also true of Victor who struggled his entire senior year and was certain that advanced math was for "astronauts." Tyronne did not apply to any colleges because of his fear of the math placement exam.

Students with positive math identities, those who rejected the label math people before Ms. Turner's honors precalculus, and the only two – Stephanie and Tamika – who never saw themselves as possessing those rare biological traits were all incapable of imagining themselves as doers of mathematics.

REFERENCES

Aguirre, J., Herbel-Eisenmann, B., Celedón-Pattichis, S., Civil, M., Wilkerson, T., Stephan, M., ... Clements, D. H. (2017). Equity within mathematics education research as a political act: Moving from choice to intentional collective professional responsibility. *Journal for Research in Mathematics Education*, 48(2), 124–147.

Anyon, J. (1997). *Ghetto schooling: A political economy of urban educational reform*. New York, NY: Teachers College, Columbia University.

Atkinson, R. C., & Geiser, S. (2009). Reflections on a century of college admissions tests. *Educational Researcher*, 38(9), 665–676. doi:10.3102/0013189X09351981

Dotson, K., & Gilbert, M. (2014). Curious disappearances: Affectability imbalances and process-based invisibility. *Hypatia*, 29, 873–888.

Ford, D. Y. (2011). Closing the achievement gap: Gifted education must join the battle. *Gifted Child Today*, 32(1), 50–53.

Freire, P. (1970). *Pedagogy of the oppressed*. New York, NY: Continuum International Publishing Group.

Gholson, M. L. (2016). Clean corners and algebra: A critical examination of the constructed invisibility of black girls and women in mathematics. *The Journal of Negro Education*, 85(3), 290–301. doi:10.7709/jnegroeducation.85.3.0290

Gutierrez, R. (2012). Context matters: How should we conceptualize equity in mathematics education? In J. Choppin, B. Herbel-Eisenmann, & D. Wagner (Eds.), *Equity in discourse for mathematics education: Theories, practices, and policies* (pp. 17–33). New York, NY: Springer.

Hanushek, E. A., Kain, J. F., & Rivkin, S. G. (2001). *Why public schools lose teachers*. Working Paper 8599. National Bureau of Economic Research, Cambridge, MA.

Harel, G. (2008). DNR perspective on mathematics curriculum and instruction: Focus on proving, part I. *Zentralblatt fuer Didaktik der Mathematik, 40*, 487–500.

Harel, G., & Koichu, B. (2010). An operational definition of learning. *The Journal of Mathematical Behavior, 29*, 115–124.

Harkness, S. S., & Stallworth, J. (2013). Photovoice: Understanding high school females' conceptions of mathematics and of learning mathematics. *Educational Studies in Mathematics, 84*, 329–347.

Liu, E., Rosenstein, J. G., Swan, A. E., & Khalil, D. (2008). When districts encounter teacher shortages: The challenges of recruiting and retaining mathematics teachers in urban districts. *Leadership and Policy in Schools, 7*, 296–323.

Martin, D. B. (2003). Hidden assumptions and unaddressed questions in *mathematics for all* in rhetoric. *The Mathematics Educator, 13*(2), 7–21.

Martin, D. B. (2012). Learning mathematics while black. *Educational Foundations*, 47–66.

McGee, E. (2013). Young, black, mathematically gifted, and stereotyped. *The High School Journal, 96*(3), 253–263.

National Council of Teachers of Mathematics. (2010). *Program for the research presession*. Reston, VA: Author.

Tatum, B. D. (2017). *"Why are all the Black kids sitting together in the cafeteria?" and other conversations about race*. New York, NY: Basic Books.

Urrieta, L., Jr (2007). Identity production in figured worlds: How some Mexican Americans become Chicana/o activist educators. *The Urban Review, 39*(2), 117–144.

Walker, E. N. (2012). *Building mathematics learning communities: Improving outcomes in urban high schools*. New York, NY: Teachers College Press.

4

WHO IS A MATH PERSON?

Every participant witnessed or experienced moments in mainstream media, their community, or the classroom that reinforced the belief that their Asian and white counterparts were superior in mathematics. It did not matter if students identified or no longer saw themselves as math people. They all acknowledged and accepted the myth of the "naturally smart" Asian or white male (Lubienski & Pinheiro, 2020, p. 7).

"THEY'RE ALWAYS GONNA DO WELL"

Shalik, on whether he thought there was a particular race associated with a math person, replied without hesitation, "Caucasian." He explained the roots of this belief below:

> ...the person holding the Guinness World Record for solving the longest math problem is Caucasian. And being around Caucasian kids, I know that they excel in math a lot. I'm not around many African Americans who do.

I reminded him that he and about 25 other Brown and Black boys and girls were enrolled in an honor's program. Again, without much hesitation or doubt, he rebutted: Oxford wanted an "honor's class so they [used] the kids that they [had]."

A little over four months into this study, Kendrick pointed at a student whom he did not know and labeled them a math person. I was standing in the back of Ms. Turner's classroom, waiting for the 12th graders to come in. There was still a handful of 11th graders finishing a quiz. One of them was sitting where Kendrick always sat. He looked at the student in question and told me that he "knew." I brought it up during our second interview:

Researcher: There was a time you were coming to class, I was already there. There was a kid sitting there, and you pointed at him and said that you "knew" he was a math person.

Kendrick: Yeah, I remember that.

Researcher: You remember that? Why did you say that?

Kendrick: Yeah, cause they always say that most Asians are good at math. They always say Asians are smarter and stuff like that.

Researcher: Do you believe that?

Kendrick: I believe it.

There was no doubt in his mind. No hesitation in his admission that one of the few Asian students enrolled at Oxford high school, 90% Black and Latinx, was a math person. Without evidence and without being prompted, he thought it was necessary for me to know what a math person looks like. Kendrick, a Jamaican native, moved to north Philadelphia only three years before the start of this study.

I think that after I came to America, like two years of being here, I was watching something, they were saying Asians and whites are smarter in math and, I never heard African Americans [mentioned]. They never talked about African Americans. They were talking like [Asians and whites] were better; but, I don't think that's true.

Researcher: Was that a movie that you were watching?

Kendrick: I think it was some TV show or something. Then, I saw it again on Family Guy. Asians are always smarter in math. They were saying like Asians are really Smart. If you're Asian, you're smart in math.

He was a bit embarrassed and uncomfortable admitting this. He digressed briefly and noncommittally – "but I don't think that's true" – midway through his account of how the myth that Asians are academically superior entered the early stages of his "Americanization."

Tamika confessed that her views of what a math person looks like were also rooted in mainstream beliefs that pervade her community and society at large.

It's just how society kinda is. It's like "oh this person is white, so they know it." Or this person is Asian, Chinese or from China, they know it. You know what I mean. And I know certain places take education more seriously but I don't know. And it's just out there so much, that's what we think because it's just out there so much. Even some times our [own] parents would say it, like "oh well they're Chinese, they're probably on top of their class." So, it's kinda instilled in us which it really shouldn't because that can be like stereotyping.

Kendrick and Tamika both wished things were different. They hoped, albeit passively and in a rather resigned tone, that there was not much credence to the notion of a racial hierarchy of math ability. They wished that their classmates, families, and the larger American society would stop promulgating the idea that whites and Asians "are always gonna do well" – a belief that was not only "instilled" in them but also critical to the type of relationship they developed – or were unable to develop – with academic learning.

Shalik, Kendrick, Tamika, and others interviewed for this book represent students whose academic development and success were premised, in part, on their ability or willingness to convince institutions, teachers, and themselves that they could fit labels or meet disciplinary expectations traditionally reserved for others.

Mainstream reform initiatives in the field, like NCTM's (2000) *Mathematic for All*, because of being so narrowly designed to bridge the so-called "achievement gap," have served to reinforce essentialist views that Black students, to experience academic success, "must become...more like white and Asian students in terms of their dispositions and values" (Martin, 2009, p. 298). Participants found nothing in K-12 mathematics education from which to draw inspiration, or imagine a story different from their presupposed inferiority compared to their white or Asian counterparts.

A GROUP OF RESILIENT CHILDREN

Most participants grew up in homes and communities that emphasized "protection against racism, pride and heritage about...the black experience, and the need to succeed within mainstream [white] America" (Strauss & Cross, 2005, p. 68). Yet, they struggled imagining possibilities outside of the widely accepted urban education tale and its assumptions about Brown and Black teenagers' intellectual aptitude and future.

Nigel identified as a math person. Like other participants, he was made aware of racial stereotypes at an early age. He grew up with a mother who stressed daily that he was not to believe in any negative assumptions about African Americans.

Nigel: My mom is heavy in this stuff cause she talked to me about it a lot.

Researcher: Heavy in what stuff?

Nigel: that racial [stereo]type stuff. She always try to say rise above it. Don't, let them put you in that stereotype cause it's not true. So, my mom always talks to me about that. That's why I took school seriously.

Nigel was a straight A student, until his senior year. He, like other participants, used the classroom as a protective cloak against anti-Black racism. Yet, he still experienced numerous instances where he had to prove to teachers and other adults that he was a "school person" or as competent as the students presumed to be academically inclined. This was particularly evident in elementary school where he was often in classes "with a lot of Asians and [whites]":

I was always running in competition [with them]. Even though I did well, [teachers] had to see it [to believe]. But, people knew they're always gonna do well. It's like, say [there are] two tests right there, [teachers] look at [white and Asian students] like, "oh I knew you got that." But, they look at me, "do you got that"?

In spite of a history of academic success, and despite being socialized to "prove them wrong," Nigel could not escape or protect himself against the myth. He too believed that his white and Asian classmates were academically superior. He was confident and had demonstrated on many occasions that he could achieve as much success as the "geniuses." However, he never refuted or rejected what his teachers taught him: white and Asian kids are "always gonna do well."

Kawhi, like Nigel, grew up in a household that was keenly aware of the importance of education. He was also raised to use academic achievement as a rebuke to disparaging views of Black Americans. During his second interview, I asked what image came to his mind when the idea of a math person is brought up:

The first thing that comes to mind is Einstein and then we're taught that Einstein is a Jewish white person...Yeah, as soon as you ask me, as soon as you ask me about it, I was like you know what, the first people that came to mind were all white. Like the first visual, even if I don't know their faces, the first visual was a bunch of white dudes in lab coats, in some Harvard classroom. That's the first thing that came to mind...And then you know because...in general you don't hear of Black mathematicians as being the geniuses in movies and TV shows or just in general.

Kawhi was not as resigned as Tamika or Kendrick in his admission. Knowingly or unwittingly, he used "revisionist history" to push back against long-standing and widespread assumptions about the intellectual and cultural superiority of whites:

I did a little bit of research...to find out [that] a lot of very, very famous white people are actually Black. If they're not Black, they are mixed-race. I believe it was Mozart, maybe Bach, I don't know, probably Mozart cause I think that he was East German...he was described as having wooly hair which is exactly the clear common sign of a Black person in that time.

He was suspicious of the fact that the biggest contributors or influencers of modern science, arts, and mathematics were all of European descent. He told me that he had come across some books and videos that suggested otherwise – he hinted at the possibility of Mozart being of African origin. Kahwi identified as a math person and was the only participant who contemplated a career in STEM. He wanted to follow in his uncle's footsteps and major in accounting. In his view, the existence and persistence of race-based beliefs in math education is part of a larger conspiracy to "keep Black people down." However, Kawhi's editorialization of historical facts and the conspiracy theories could not rival or challenge a "bunch of white dudes in lab coats" as the accepted and expected image of doers of mathematics.

Like Kawhi and Nigel, Stephanie viewed being Black in this country as a fight to reverse negative images and narratives associated with African Americans:

There're multiple stereotypes. But, it seems as though we always get stuck with the negative ones. For some odd reason – that's just how the world works, we always get stuck with the negative ones. So, we have to work twice as hard as any other race to show that we are the opposite of what they may see on TV, or what they may see on videos.

However, she also expressed frustrations for always having to be better than average and to show the world otherwise:

Sometimes it stresses me because that means I try to put more pressure on myself. Especially when you're around different

minorities and sometimes different minorities come off as though
they know more than you. They may not say it, but their demeanor,
the way they come off is as though "I know more than you do."
And, I'm not saying that every race is like that but you can tell. And
the first thing you think of is because of race. Why would you look
[me] and think you know more than [me] – race. So, honestly I put
more stress on myself because I feel like you have to put twice as
more effort in showing them that I know as much as [they] know if
not more. You're putting more pressure on yourself which is not a
bad thing because at the end, you always come out with a good
outcome.

Kendrick also echoed the other participants' sense of social responsibility at it relates to race and academic performance. He went even further and explained that being strong and being better than average were necessary to prove to the world that Black people are "normal." Kendrick ended his second interview detailing what he meant:

We're a minority but we're normal, we're here, we're doing the
same thing, we can achieve the same thing everybody's achieving…
we're just a minority but we're the same like everybody else.

Participants developed belief systems and worldviews that helped them navigate and negotiate their position in society. They were socialized to excel academically. Their motivation stemmed from a perceived social responsibility to write a counterstory to widely accepted and uncontested notions of the academic inferiority of Black Americans.

However, rewriting the narrative of Black and Brown students' academic aptitude and prospects did not and could not extend to mathematics.

BELONGING

A surprising pattern emerged out of this study. Nine out of 11 students interviewed for this book were unwilling or unable to name other students in Ms. Turner's class as math people. This was true of participants who identified as math people during the time of the interviews; it was also the case for those who no longer identified or never saw themselves as math people. It's important to reiterate here that most of the students in Ms. Tuner's class and the college pipeline program had been in the same math and English classes for at least two consecutive years.

Researcher: Do you know of any friends either here or outside of here who are math people?

Tamika: (She signed heavily).

Researcher: Would you call let's say Weldon [the school valedictorian and a close friend] a math person?

Tamika: I'm not sure.

Researcher: But do you think that he would consider himself a math person?

Tamika: I think that he would consider himself a math person because he's not too strong in writing. Usually, people always think like "oh you're not a math person, you have to be a writer." If you're not a writer, you have to be math. I think that he will consider himself one; but I probably wouldn't.

This was not the first or only documented instance of Tamika refusing to acknowledge Weldon's academic achievements. Earlier in this book, I discussed how she invalidated his valedictorian title – along with her and other students' classroom successes – by attributing it to widespread cheating and nepotism at Oxford. In the excerpt above, she characterized, and in some ways reduced, Weldon's positive identification with mathematics to more of an emotional, knee-jerk response to his struggles with writing. As mentioned before, Tamika and Weldon were close friends. Most days, they drove to and away from school together. They were often absent on the same days. They knew each other really well in and outside of the classroom.

I see teachers helping a lot of people there and you know with me, I'm not gonna lie, she used to help me…So, me and Weldon, we had this conversation, talking about him going into nursing and stuff. I mean they talk about the math classes that we have to take [in college]. I asked him "well would you be ready for that?" And he's like "well, I'm good in math, blah, blah." And I have to be realistic. Professors there are not gonna be helping us…I think people think that I'm trying to be negative but I'm just really trying to be realistic.

Her unwillingness or inability to label Weldon a math person or to accept the fact that he was the school's highest performer was puzzling. It is an example of how long-standing and rigid assumptions about academic labels and "to whom they should be applied" can obfuscate experiences (Appiah, 2018, p. 12).

Tamika could not assign the exclusive label "math person" to her close friend, nor could she see him as a "legitimate" school valedictorian because she had "to be realistic." A reality trapped in the conventional wisdom that views schools like Oxford as "failure," and that describes its majority Black and Brown student body and the surrounding underserved community as part of a "culture of poverty."

> Master narratives operate internally – we compare our lives to the stories we know...They are, then, widely circulating in the culture, not only in obvious "story" forms (movies, literature, television) but also in our accounts of our own and each others' lives...they accumulate familiarity and clarity while blurring and erasing plot elements that don't fit.
>
> (Romeo & Stewart, 1999, p. XIV)

She did not and would not see her classmates' achievements as evidence that they were "ready" to lead productive postsecondary lives. In her eyes, high point averages or being in honor's precalculus at Oxford high school should be assessed with a caveat; they should be measured against "the social types that [are expected to] populate" academic disciplines and lead successful lives (Urrieta, 2007, p. 108). Tamika, like other participants, was very familiar with those "social types." They did not attend or live near schools like Oxford. Their success stories did not match hers. In fact, from Tamika's perspective, master narratives about the ideal or promising student were not only incompatible to high grade point averages at Oxford, but also they made her secondary education feel fraudulent or cheap; they rendered other participants' academic history delegitimate.

Unlike Tamika, Andre viewed himself and classmates in a more positive and optimistic light. He showed very little interest in honor's precalculus. In fact, during his first interview, he conceded that he never studied or spent much time on homework. He was late often – but never absent. He typically strolled in 10–15 minutes after the bell rang the beginning of class, always trailing Nigel. Ms. Turner described Andre as "a once very good student." Indeed, during the times that he and I worked one on one or in small groups, it was obvious that he was either very familiar with the honor's precalculus curriculum or had a very strong background in algebraic thinking and manipulations. Andre caught up on concepts or procedures rather quickly and without much difficulty, regardless of the level of abstraction or sophistication (e.g., simplifying complex expressions like $\frac{x-2}{3x-1}$). He walked around with an unmistakable air of self-assuredness.

Researcher: Do you have friends who are math people?

Andre: Uh, I don't know, probably like simple common math. You know like dealing with money and you know how to count. Everybody knows how to count.

Researcher: Anyone as passionate about math as you? Anyone you know?

Andre: Nah, they probably don't think much of it.

Researcher: Why do you think that there aren't more people in the classroom who share the same passion you have for math?

Andre: The classroom that we're in now? I guess everyone [is a math person] cause it's an optional course.

Researcher: So, would you say that everybody in this class is as passionate as you?

Andre: As passionate as me? I'mma put myself ahead of everybody. Nobody's on the same level as me. I'm not saying that I'm the smartest kid in the class but I'm saying that I'm the most passionate about math.

Researcher: Why do you think that there aren't more people like you in the classroom?

Andre: I don't know. I don't really talk to anyone.

Andre believed that he was a math person – not only because he had success in math classrooms but also because he was "passionate" – a belief that he maintained in spite of his struggles or disinterest in honor's precalculus. He said, somewhat flippantly and dismissively, that every student in Ms. Turner's class had to be a math person because they elected to enroll in an elective, a course that was not required for graduation. However, when asked to identify classmates who fitted his definition of a math person, he could not – would not.

Andre had been with most of the students observed for this book for at least two consecutive academic years. He was classmate or friends with many participants for most of or his entire secondary mathematics education – he and Nigel were inseparable. Nonetheless, he did not know anyone well enough to determine if they had the requisite "passion" to be a math person:

...someone is going to assume [you're not a math person]. Black people, I don't know why, but they never put us on a pedestal. So, I guess you gotta show them more. It's another motivation thing.

Like other participants, Andre was acutely aware of race-based stereotypes surrounding mathematics. He used them as "motivation." However, that motivation and his acknowledgment that Black people were "never put on a pedestal" did not feature anywhere in his commentary on classmates' mathematical aptitude. In fact, his initial response to whether he would label any friends or students in Ms. Turner's class math people was "no." Instead, he explained that some may be able to excel in "simple common math," but, in his estimation, no one in honor's precalculus or at Oxford had the "passion" to be put on a "pedestal."

Kendrick was the only participant who named classmates in the honor's precalculus class whom he believed to be math people:

> *Researcher: How many people would you say in this class, in Ms. Turner's class are math people?*
>
> *Kendrick: Uhm (thinking)*
>
> *Researcher: Or anyone you know for sure that this person is a math person?*
>
> *Kendrick: ...Tamika or Weldon, you can see that they know their stuff. Who else? I don't know. Those two.*

Kendrick hesitated. He needed further prompting. However, he did identify Tamika and Weldon. His response stemmed from the countless times he witnessed them on the board solving problems or at their desks answering and asking thoughtful questions. He alluded to this in his response: "you can see that they know their stuff." He listed a series of factual assertions for why Weldon and Tamika could fit the label "math people." However, as discussed previously, Kendrick did not need any evidence, nor did he provide an explanation for proclaiming a junior of Vietnamese background, whom he did not know, a member of the community of math people.

"I AM NOT THE TYPE"

For many participants, the presumed relationship between academic competence and identity was fraught with inconsistencies. Kawhi, who had the highest score on Cecil B. Moore University's math placement exams, was one of the few participants who considered a STEM career. He decided on accounting because he was determined not to repeat his mother's "mistakes" and ongoing financial struggles. He, too, could not identify any other students in Ms. Turner's class as math people.

The absence or underrepresentation of people of African descent in the history and evolution of mathematics or science which he decried as a racist ploy did not feature anywhere in his evaluation of the mathematical aptitude of his Brown and Black teenage classmates. Kawhi did not only fail to identify anyone else in Ms. Turner's honor's precalculus as a math person, but also he was unaware and unphased by the omission – this was in stark contrast to how he reacted earlier in the same interview to confessing that his image of a math person was that of "white dudes in lab coats." There was a misalignment between Kawhi's Afrocentric proclivities and his own relationship to the existence of a math person as the mythical Asian or white male.

Kawhi drew a rather peculiar distinction between being "comfortable" pursuing a math-oriented profession and *belonging* to the community of math people.

> *I'm just good at [math]. I'm not the type of person that's going into accounting because I love it. I'm going because the profession itself and the career itself is one that is comfortable with me at least…as far as working…with numbers.*

When prompted to expand on the need for the distinction, he explained:

> *I think for you to be someone like that, in that kind of community, you have to dive into it and be a part of it. If you're thinking about a community situation, like the only communities that I have ever been a part of are the ones that I dive into…I think that if I were a person who constantly was looking for new ways to develop in mathematics, then I would come across more people that help me do that.*

The discordance in Kawhi's relationship to mathematics is an illustration of the tension that can exist between *actual* identity and a *designated* identity:

> *The reifying, significant narratives about a person can be split into two subsets: actual identity, consisting of stories about the actual state of affairs, and designated identity, consisting of narratives presenting a state of affairs which, for one reason or another, is expected to be the case, if not now, then in the future.*
>
> (Sfard & Prusak, 2005, p. 18)

His conviction that mathematics was his most "comfortable" subject was based on a history of "actual" classroom successes. Kawhi's decision to pursue accounting was grounded in "factual assertions" about his mathematical aptitude (p. 18). However, he could not see himself as already "a part of" the community of math people. He felt compelled to create a separation and distance between "being good with numbers" and fitting or assuming the designated identity of a math person, traditionally reserved for a few "great thinkers." Likewise, he was actively engaged in "rewriting" history so that it could be more representative of people who look like him; but, he was unable to imagine his classmates as belonging to the community of math people.

CONCLUSION

Students' conception of a math person as someone born with "math genes" played a critical role into the construction of their own math identities. Every participant, regardless of their identification with mathematics, experienced moments that reified the belief that a math person was either an Asian or white male. Some rejected their academic achievements or dismissed their classmates' classroom successes. Others built a wall of separation between positive classroom experiences and belonging.

Ernst and Young and Cecil B. Moore University's partnership provided honor students an educational experience and resources superior than that of other Oxford students. However, the honor's program could not inoculate them from pervasive racist ideologies enmeshed in mathematics education; it was not successful in protecting participants' academic identity development against the existence and persistence of the urban education tale.

Focusing this book on a group of honors students from Oxford challenges and departs from dominant storylines about race-comparative approaches to explaining the opportunity gap in the field of mathematics education. Students' "lived experience...[was] key to understanding the cultural and sociological" processes (Richardson, 1997, p. 67) that contribute to the existence and persistence of racial inequality in mathematics education.

REFERENCES

Appiah, K. A. (2018). *The lies that bind: Rethinking identity, creed, country, color.* New York, NY: W. W. Norton & Company.

Lubienski, P., & Pinheiro, W. A. (2020). Gender and mathematics: What can other disciplines tell us? What is our role? *Journal of Urban Mathematics Education, 13*(1), 1–14. doi:10.21423/jume-v13i1a377

Martin, D. B. (2009). Researching race in mathematics education. *Teachers College Record, 111*(2), 295–338.

National Council of Teachers of Mathematics. (2000). *Principles and standards for school mathematics.* Reston, VA: Author.

Richardson, L. (1997). *Fields of play: Constructing an academic life.* New Brunswick, NJ: Rutgers University Press.

Romeo, M., & Stewart, A. J. (Eds.). (1999), *Women's untold stories: Breaking silence, talking back, voicing complexity.* New York, NY: Routledge.

Sfard, A., & Prusak, A. (2005). Telling identities: In search of an analytical tool for investigating learning as a culturally shaped activity. *Educational Researcher, 34*(4), 14–22.

Strauss, L. C., & Cross, W. E., Jr (2005). Transacting black identity: A two-week daily-diary study. In G. Downey, J. S. Eccles, & C. M. Chatman (Eds.), *Navigating the future: Social identity, coping, and life tasks* (pp. 67–95). New York, NY: Russell Sage Foundation.

Urrieta, L., Jr (2007). Identity production in figured worlds: How some Mexican Americans become Chicana/o activist educators. *The Urban Review, 39*(2), 117–144.

5

ACADEMIC IDENTITY AS BELONGING

This chapter takes a closer look at the idea of *academic identity* defined as a sense of *belonging*. Previous sections of this book focused on participants' academic identity development within the context of the urban education tale and in relationship to master narratives surrounding and controlling "what is" and "who" can be a math person. Here, I provide the rationale for identity as belonging as a perspective and framework with which to analyze the interplay between classroom experiences, students' perception of mathematics education, and their self-formulations in response to the binary math person-everyone else.

The works of philosopher Kwame A. Appiah and poet and scholar Eli C. Goldblatt helped to delineate the concept of math identity as belonging. They helped to elucidate what 11 Black students, who do not fit the label or image of what/who is a math person, had to contend with, in classrooms, academic institutions, in their communities and society, in figuring out whether they could ever become members of the community of doers of mathematics.

IDENTITY AS BELONGING

Appiah's (2018) *The Lies That Bind: Rethinking Identity* explains how notions of identity, whether based on religion, nationality, socioeconomic status, race, or culture, are premised on "misconceptions" and falsehoods (p. xvi). The "lies" that both connect and divide us also inform and distort our self-conceptions, our worldview. They form the basis for our relationship to the world. Identities,

*...once they get their grip on us, command us.... If [we] do not care
for the shapes [our] identities have taken, [we] cannot simply refuse
them; they are not [ours] alone.*

(pp. 217–218)

The book opens with anecdotal accounts of the author in the back of taxis, in different countries and on various continents, trying to offer a satisfactory response to "where are you from?" Almost everywhere he went, his answer was received with suspicion and disbelief. Appiah is of mixed race – the progeny of a Ghanaian father and of a white English mother – and with somewhat "ambiguous" physical features. He was mistaken for Ethiopian in Rome, Brazilian in São Paulo, and Indian in his birthplace of London (p. xi). The facts about his existence and origins, in his interlocutors' eyes, did not match his appearance, diction, and name. Those facts created a dissonance in the taxi drivers' understanding and frame of reference as it pertains "to whom [the 'Londoner identity'] should be applied" (p. 12).

The stories and lies that define and limit membership to what and who is a "Londoner" also serve to establish a specific English identity and to distinguish it from other national identities. Likewise, long-standing beliefs that undergird a given discipline and its academic practices come with an archetype, a fixed idea and image of the ideal learner (in Chapter 2, I used 2020 presidential nominee Andrew Yang, a political science major in college and a lawyer by profession, to show how he used his Asian background to pose as a math person during his campaign without explanation or push back). Those who do not fit that image, like Appiah and the label Londoner, have to grapple with ongoing tension and negotiations between their self-concepts and a *designated identity*, a tradition that formulates, and even regulates, what it means to possess a certain identity (Sfard & Prusak, 2005, p. 18). They have to make sense of life experiences and personal stories in relationship to enduring narratives often exclusive or derogatory of them.

LEARNING AS BECOMING

Learning, here, is viewed as a tangle of institutionalized practices and ongoing identity work that, for some students, is integral to and necessary for academic growth and success. A fitting illustration is Goldblatt's (1995) case study of three high school students who, in their quest to develop greater fluency with the rules governing academic writing, find themselves in a fight for *authority* and membership. Goldblatt observed that focusing on the concept of authority made it possible to study

> *...classic writing problems not as an indication of personal ignorance of "grammar rules" but as a function of social relations between author and sponsor.*
>
> *(p. 152)*

Writing, for those three students, extended beyond acquisition of skills, ability, and pedagogy. Activities like punctuating a sentence, revising a paragraph's structure, or reviewing conventions carried deeper and more ominous meanings. The pervasiveness of the archetypical writer image not only complicated students' relationship with writing but also led them to view their "private selves," the facts about their existence and origins, as hindrance or antithetical to becoming an author. The three students in Golblatt's study had to negotiate belonging to a tradition that, at least subliminally, compelled them to "blot out their private selves in order to gain some modicum of public acceptance," institutional sponsorship, and membership (p. 152).

As an individual matures into adolescence and adulthood, their need to belong to a specific group and to be distinct from the rest of the world (including that group) becomes more salient (Chatman, Eccles, & Malanchuck, 2005, p. 120). In the case of Black and Brown teenagers, omnipresent reminders about their differences – often disparaged – compared to the white majority, force them to take on the "additional developmental task of considering race and ethnicity in their identity formation" (pp. 120–121). One can claim allegiance to different socioeconomic groups over a lifetime. However, there is no eluding the *social imaginary* or "discursive space...in which [Black, Indigenous, and People of Color] are already constructed, imagined, and positioned" (Ibrahim, 1999, p. 353).

The three students in question, like the participants observed and interviewed for this book, hailed from racially and socioeconomically isolated communities of color in Philadelphia. They are part of the "urban education tale," the American social imaginary, that views, treats, and teaches Black and Brown teenagers to think of themselves, and their community, as anti-intellectuals and averse to schooling (Ogbu, 1992; Youdell, 2003). Academic identity as belonging to a community of practice allows for a shift away from the "ability model" – a few are expected to succeed and others need to try harder – and the narrow conception of learning as acquisition of skills.

DOING MATH, A SOCIALIZATION PROCESS

Focusing this book on students' stories of belonging made it possible to explore the limits imposed by long-standing, yet understudied, assumptions about "who" and "what" is a *math person*. Math identity as belonging is grounded in Appiah's (2018) conception of identities as long-established lies that define, stratify, and confine us. Goldblatt's (1995) critical exploration of academic writing as a process of inclusion or exclusion served as a model for how to investigate the perniciousness and restrictive forces of narratives predicated on deficit-laden beliefs about certain groups. These two works, in spite of being separated by more than two decades and discrete disciplinary norms, combined to explain and anchor the idea of doing mathematics as a *socialization* process – a learning experience in which success depends, in significant part, on a student having to perform and assume the "*normative identity* [of] a doer of mathematics" formulated by the discipline and regulated through academic practices (Cobb, Gresalfi, & Hodge, 2008, p. 4). Mathematics classrooms, in spite of being conceived as neutral or value-free, socialize students, relatively early in their academic journey, into believing in a fixed conception of who and what is a math person. Students, through the ongoing cycle of engaging with mathematical tasks and teacher feedback, develop a sense of whether they are or can ever become members of the high-status and exclusive discipline.

The field of mathematics education is replete with studies on Black students' underperformance or lack of motivation compared to their white and Asian counterparts. Berry, Pinter, and McClain (2013) observed that the "implicit message [from those studies] is that Black children are not worth studying in their own right and that a comparison group is necessary" (p. 45). The race-based comparison approach and the disproportionate number of studies focused on Black students' "failure" have helped to establish a reality and expectations surrounding who can be successful in mathematics and who cannot. This perception has colored teachers' attitudes toward Black students; it has also shaped students' appraisal of their potential and abilities.

One of the most frequently referenced explanations for why Black students trail their Asian and white counterparts in academic attainments is the belief that the former group is burdened by a fear of *acting white*. A fear described as being unique to African Americans who choose not to invest requisite time and effort into their education because of a concern that others would view them as passing for white. Tyson, Darity, and Castellino (2005) dispelled the acting white theory and questioned its empirical merit and origins. In their study of eight high schools in North Carolina, they found that the majority of high-achieving Black students had no fear of acting white; some avoided advanced classes simply out of fear of lowering their grade point average. The authors observed that the "burden of acting white" is only present in some schools "under certain conditions" (p. 583). Conditions, like *tracking* and "gifted" programs, that often separate students by race and socioeconomic status (p.

600; see Anyon, 1997; Oakes, 1985), thereby suggesting to students in near racially homogeneous classrooms that there exists an image of the ideal or academically inclined learner.

The key findings of Tyson et al. are consistent with students' narratives collected for this book. Every Black student observed and interviewed for this book was incredibly motivated to succeed academically and professionally. The problem was that, in spite of their being enrolled in an honor's mathematics class, and despite considerable overall academic success, they were unable to transfer any of it into their relationships to mathematics.

To be clear, avoidance or fear of mathematics is not unique to Black Americans. Learners around the globe have reported feelings or experiencing *math anxiety* (e.g., Wilson, 2014). Nonetheless, the key finding here is that the limited range of possible identities available to this study's participants prevented them from even contemplating membership into the community of math people. They were determined to use schooling as protection against anti-Black racism; their determination did not extent to mathematics education, nor could it be translated into STEM careers.

Centering this study around a group of highly motivated Black students in an honor's program sought to reject a tradition rooted in racist ideologies. Participants' unique stories and perspectives about mathematics education amplify calls to not only abandon but also rewrite the narrative of Black students' "failure [in mathematics] as normative" or expected (Martin, 2012, p. 48). Their voices bring coherence and substance to a different story – one that offers new insights about racial inequality in mathematics education and that allows space for new possibilities in discussing and addressing the race-based opportunity gap.

SHIFTING AWAY FROM A TRADITION

The field of social cognitive psychology has been instrumental in generating insights on the immediate and long-term impact of interpersonal and institutional racism. However, making sense of race-based differences in mathematics education requires greater focus on and deeper understanding of students' identity construction within the context and in response to learning environments, disciplinary norms, curricula, instructions, and academic activities.

I contend that widespread adoption of *self-efficacy* in educational research has constrained contemporary conceptions and understanding of academic performance. Self-efficacy is defined as an individual's "convictions in their own effectiveness" (Bandura, 1977, p. 193; see also Bandura, 1986); it has led to an extensive literature in STEM education focused on individuals' "efficacy beliefs" and its impact on their academic and career prospects (Pajares, 1996, pp. 551–552). The ubiquity of efficacy beliefs in education has given rise to other related social cognitive constructs such as "academic motivation," "outcome expectations," and "self-regulation" which have become common-place in studies attempting to draw connections between students' dispositions or emotions and their cognitive processes. My contention is that reliance on concepts like self-efficacy and its correlates (e.g., motivation) to explain aca-demic performance can help perpetuate deficit-oriented and essentialist expla-nations for the existence and persistence of racial differences in students' academic attainments.

Theories and frameworks based on the presupposed link between compe-tence and academic confidence, in the case of this study's participants, are simply inadequate and incomplete. Psychologists, educational researchers, and practitioners have long debated whether academic performance "and confi-dence go hand in hand" (Burton, 2004, p. 357). Burton (2004) argued that, in spite of the absence of a consensus on an operational definition for constructs like self-confidence or self-efficacy, the belief that "success in mathematics breeds confidence" has dominated mainstream beliefs about learning and teaching (p. 357). The 11 stories that made this book possible not only refute the notion that academic success in a discipline leads to positive identification but they also suggest that there is a

> ...need to gain greater insights into the ways students speak about the construct of confidence, in what contexts they do so, and how they pair confidence with other notions, such as a sense of belonging or community.
>
> (Darragh, 2013, p. 218)

For the honor's students who participated in this study, identification with mathematics became about belonging to a tradition that always excluded and treated them as failures. It was about claiming allegiance to a "great thinkers" community where people of African descent were never expected or welcomed.

CONCLUSION

A number of scholars have recentered attention on Black students' "brilliant," successful, and diverse experiences with mathematics (Berry et al., 2013, p. 45; see also Berry, 2005, 2008; Jett, 2010; Martin, 2000; McGee, 2013; McGee & Martin, 2011a, 2011b; Noble, 2011; Stinson, 2013; Walker, 2012). This study, focusing on an honor's precalculus classroom at Oxford high school, an urban and underresourced public school of predominantly African American students – 57% Black and 33% Latinx – joins in this growing movement.

This book challenges the field of mathematics education's neutrality and its claim to universality. It joins others in sounding the alarm on the perniciousness and pervasiveness of narratives premised on the intellectual inferiority of racial or ethnic groups like Black Americans and on the unwillingness of reform and policy initiatives in the field of mathematics education to confront the disciplines' racist roots and exclusionary practices.

REFERENCES

Anyon, J. (1997). *Ghetto schooling: A political economy of urban educational reform.* New York, NY: Teachers College, Columbia University.

Appiah, K. A. (2018). *The lies that bind: Rethinking identity, creed, country, color.* New York, NY: W. W. Norton & Company.

Bandura, A. (1977). Self efficacy: Toward a unifying theory of behavioral change. *Psychological Review, 84*(2), 191–215.

Bandura, A. (1986). *Social foundations of thought and action: A social cognitive theory.* Englewood Cliffs, NJ: Prentice Hall.

Berry, R. (2005). Voices of success: Descriptive portraits of two successful African American male middle school mathematics students. *Journal of African American Studies, 8*(4), 46–62.

Berry, R. (2008). Access to upper-level mathematics: The stories of successful African American middle school boys. *Journal for Research in Mathematics Education, 39*(5), 464–488.

Berry, R. Q., Pinter, H. H., & McClain, O. L. (2013). A critical review of K-12 mathematics education, 1900-present. In J. Leonard & D. B. Martin (Eds.), *The brilliance of Black children in mathematics: Beyond the numbers and toward new discourse* (pp. 23–53). Charlotte, NC: Information Age Publishing.

Burton, L. (2004). "Confidence is everything": Perspectives of teachers and students on learning mathematics. *Journal of Mathematics Teacher Education, 7*, 357–381.

Chatman, C. M., Eccles, J. S., & Malanchuk, O. (2005). Identity negotiation in everyday setting. In G. Downey, J. S. Eccles, & C. M. Chatman (Eds.),

Navigating the future: Social identity, coping, and life tasks (pp. 116–139). New York, NY: Russell Sage Foundation.

Cobb, P., Gresalfi, M., & Hodge, L. H. (2008). An interpretive scheme for analyzing the identities that students develop in mathematics classrooms. *Journal for Research in Mathematics Education, 39,* 1–29.

Darragh, L. (2013). Constructing confidence and identities of belonging in mathematics at the transition to secondary school. *Research in Mathematics Education, 15*(3), 215–229.

Goldblatt, E. C. (1995). *'Round my way: Authority and double-consciousness in three urban high school writers.* Pittsburgh, PA: University of Pittsburgh Press.

Ibrahim, A. E. K. M. (1999). Becoming black: Rap and hip hop, race, gender, identity, and the politics of ESL learning. *TESOL Quarterly, 33*(3), 349–369.

Jett, C. (2010). "Many are called, but few are chosen": The role of spirituality and religion in the educational outcomes of "chosen" African American male mathematics majors. *The Journal of Negro Education, 79*(3), 324–334.

Martin, D. B. (2000). *Mathematics success and failure among African-American youth: The roles of sociohistorical context, community forces, school influence, and individual agency.* New York, NY: Routledge.

Martin, D. B. (2012). Learning mathematics while Black. *The Journal of Educational Foundations, 26,* 47–66.

McGee, E. (2013). Young, Black, mathematically gifted, and stereotyped. *The High School Journal, 96*(3), 253–263.

McGee, E., & Martin, D. (2011a). From the hood to being hooded: A case study of a Black male PhD. *Journal of African American Males, 2,* 46–65.

McGee, E., & Martin, D. (2011b). You would not believe what I have to go through to prove my intellectual value! Stereotype management among successful Black college mathematics and engineering students. *American Educational Research Journal, 48,* 1347–1389.

Noble, R. (2011). Mathematics self-efficacy and African American male students: An examination of models of success. *Journal of African American Males in Education, 2*(2), 188–213.

Oakes, J. (1985). *Keeping track: How schools structure inequality.* New Haven, CT: Yale University Press.

Ogbu, J. U. (1992). Understanding cultural diversity and learning. *Educational Researcher, 21*(8), 5–24.

Pajares, F. (1996). Self-efficacy beliefs in academic settings. *Review of Educational Research, 66*(4), 543–578.

Sfard, A., & Prusak, A. (2005). Telling identities: In search of an analytical tool for investigating learning as a culturally shaped activity. *Educational Researcher, 34*(4), 14–22.

Stinson, D. W. (2013). Negotiating the "white male math myth": African American male students and success in school mathematics. *Journal for Research in Mathematics Education, 44*(1), 69–99. doi:10.5951/jresematheduc.44.1.0069

Tyson, K., Darity, W. J., & Castellino, D. R. (2005). It's not "a black thing": Understanding the burden of acting white and other dilemmas of high achievement. *American Sociological Review, 70*(4), 582–605.

Walker, E. N. (2012). *Building mathematics learning communities: Improving outcomes in urban high schools.* New York, NY: Teachers College Press.

Wilson, S. (2014). "Fail at maths and you fail at life": Learned barriers to equal opportunities. *International Public Health Journal, 6*(2), 147–160.

Youdell, D. (2003). Identity traps or how black students fail: The interactions between biographical, sub-cultural, and learner identities. *British Journal of Sociology of Education, 24*(1), 3–20.

6

A LOOK AT RACIAL EQUITY IN MATHEMATICS EDUCATION

*There is no singular, essential characterization [of being Black].
[Black students] come from varied socioeconomic and family
backgrounds and respond to schooling and education in multiple
ways. However, given that the meanings for Blackness have always
permeated the prevailing racial ideologies, institutional practices,
social arrangements, and opportunity structures in the U.S. society
(Bonilla-Silva, 2001), these meanings are no less relevant to Black
children's mathematical development and lived realities.*

(Martin, 2012, p. 50)

The 11 Black teenage boys and girls observed and interviewed for this book
made clear that there is "no singular" or all-encompassing Black story. Each
one and the collection of their voices, journeys in K-12, perspectives, and
relationships to the idea of a math person complicated – thus deepened –
existing understandings surrounding racial inequality in mathematics education. Their individual stories showed the depths of "prevailing racial ideologies" in academic learning. They offered much needed insights into the
pernicious and limiting impact of mainstream beliefs premised on the intellectual inferiority of Black Americans.

One of the more troubling themes that emerged out of this study is participants' shared unwillingness or inability to seek, accept, or even contemplate
the possibility of belonging to the community of doers of mathematics. In spite
of being the most praised and best supported students at Oxford high school,
they could not imagine or entertain fitting the "genius" label – some, like

Tamika and Stephanie, even rejected the idea of being "promising" students. Despite being raised to value and purpose academic achievements as an antiracist project, they found nothing in mathematics education, nothing in Ernst and Young and Cecil B. Moore's college pipeline program that inspired or motivated them to translate their schooling history, drive, and perceived social responsibility into membership to the exclusive club of great thinkers. There were no opportunities in their K-12 math classroom experiences that connected or extended their fight against anti-Blackness in education to mathematics' racist legacy.

This chapter seeks to expand on this very issue. It offers a critical evaluation of racial equity in mathematics education as a context with which to better understand the identities that participants developed in response to the mythical race-based hierarchy of math ability.

This section of the book focuses on key mainstream reform movements that dominated the field in the twentieth century and that continue to shape classrooms and curricula. I show how those efforts, rooted in market-based ideologies and based primarily on the assumed neutrality of mathematics, have failed to generate adequate resources, insights, and political will to address mathematics' legacy of racial exclusion. As a result, this study's participants reached the end of their K-12 education unequipped or unwilling to continue to wrestle with enduring race-based and widespread "narrow interpretations of the talented mathematics student" (Walker, 2012, p. 112).

This chapter does not portend to provide an exhaustive and detailed history of mathematics education. Other scholars, like Berry, Pinter, & McClain, 2013; Herrera & Owens, 2001; Klein, 2003; and Schoenfeld, 2002, 2004, 2016, provide a more complete history of K-12 mathematics and of the events that bore and shaped the 1990s "math wars." However, this part of the book underscores the failure of a century-old debate to embrace race-based equity as a core and guiding principle and some the resulting impact on racial inequality in mathematics education.

The discipline's insistence on being defined by universal standards and our overreliance on math scores as an objective measure of intelligence (and a gatekeeper to professional pathways) has made it harder for a great number of students to explore and engage with a

> ...much broader view of mathematics as an evolving, innovative science of patterns, relations, and logical reasoning and not just a set of rules for the manipulation of numbers and symbols to be memorized.
>
> (Sheffield, 2017, p. 14)

A century of short-sighted and short-lived initiatives in the field of mathematics education left this study's participants in an untenable position. They were alone, in the midst of the normal pressures and uncertainties of post-secondary life, trying to figure out ways to form meaningful or even just functional relationships with mathematics and a community of geniuses who purportedly never looked and lived like them.

BRIEF HISTORY OF MATHEMATICS EDUCATION

Mathematics education "came together as a discipline" in the 1960s–70s, in the middle of momentous political and social unrests (Schoenfeld, 2016, p. 505). A wide range of protest movements (e.g., Women Liberation Movement, Civil Rights Movement, Gay Rights Movement) challenged and, in some instances, initiated drastic – long overdue – and lasting changes to many facets of American life. A rich "radical political tradition" was born (Hall, 2008) and earned the 1960s a prominent place in modern American history. The ripple effects on public education were palpable and shaped many aspects of K-12 curricula. For instance,

> ...courses in black history and culture became far more commonplace, at least for a time, reflecting a surge of interest in those topics on college campuses [and secondary education classrooms]....
>
> (Rury & Hill, 2013, pp. 487–488)

However, the field of mathematics education remained largely unaffected. The mainstream and institutionally sponsored debates that surrounded mathematics instruction during that time were motivated and guided by one "dominant social narrative" – Sputnik (Schoenfeld, 2016, p. 504).

Black youth's relentless pressure on academic institutions to value and include African American culture in K-12 and higher education stayed in the margins of public discourses about teaching and learning mathematics. Berry et al. (2013) observed that, in response to Sputnik, efforts and initiatives to reform mathematics focused on

> ...a select few communities and students [who] were to be served by the "new math" reform. The appeal to limit the mathematics reform to the perceived "best and brightest" was built on a political philosophy focused on protecting the national security and interests of America (Tate, 1997). This meant that the mathematics experiences

*of Black children were largely ignored and pushed aside within the
larger discussions of* Sputnik.

(p. 30)

America's concerns about lagging behind rival nations in science and
mathematics did not include racial equity. Black students' roaring condem-
nation of institutional policies and practices that have adversely affected
"critical aspects of their lives" (Rury & Hill, 2013, p. 487) was deemed
outside of the purview of the country's immediate and long-term plans to
maintain global competitiveness. Math classrooms were impervious to the
1960s explosion of social, cultural, and political activism. Mathematics education was not only unscathed, but the field's birth and subsequent evolution
remained anchored in a stubborn allegiance to universality, and a tradition
prided on exclusivity.

Mathematics education underwent many major epistemic and curricular
transformations between the middle of the last century and the beginning of
the twenty-first century. By the 1950s, the progressive education movement
that dominated the first decades of the century was deemed a failure and
responsible for the alarming number of students graduating high school
"unprepared" for college or the workforce. As mentioned earlier, the former
Soviet Union's successful launch of *Sputnik*, the first space satellite, was
viewed as a major embarrassment by most American media. The public
interpreted *Sputnik* as evidence that science and mathematics instructions in
the United States were in dire need of reform (Klein, 2003, p. 184). A *new
math* movement emerged, promoting more rigor in K-12 curricula and an
emphasis on comprehension over computation. This was short-lived. A decade
later, public and government support for the "new math" waned due to, in
large part, "a 10-year decline in Scholastic Aptitude Test (SAT) scores" and
dissenters' convictions that a "back-to-basics" overhaul was what mathematics education needed (Herrera & Owens, 2001, p. 87; see Usiskin, 1985).
The end of the twentieth century was marked by the publications of *A Nation
at Risk* (1983), NCTM's (1989) *Curriculum and Evaluation Standards for
School Mathematics*, and the resurgence of mainstream appetite for progressive ideas (e.g., Constructivism, Open Education Movement). The confluence
of those events reinvigorated and reoriented the debate over what it means to
teach and learn mathematics. The chasm between those, mostly mathematicians, who sought to affirm and conserve the "identity" of mathematics and
educational reformers interested in renovating math education, especially for
K-12 grew in intensity and popularity in the latter half of the twentieth
century.

CASUALTIES OF THE "MATH WARS"

Decades of tense disagreements, polarizing reform and policy initiatives, and uninspiring results in students' performance culminated into the 1990s *math wars*. Irreconcilable differences about the pedagogical merit of skills-based versus process-oriented methods of instruction were at the center of the wars. The *cognitive revolution* of the 1970s and 80s and its wave of "new ways of understanding knowledge, thinking, and learning" fueled the math wars; it unearthed many "problems" with how students were learning mathematics, but offered no concrete solutions (Schoenfeld, 2004, pp. 11–12). The math wars became proxy wars for the two major political parties in America – liberals and conservatives – and ammunition for renewed partisan rhetoric. Politicians were summoned to act. The US Secretary of Education of the time, Richard Riley, attempted to do just that; he quickly became "the focus of the very…wars he sought to quell" (Klein, 2003, p. 176). The math wars garnered mainstream attention and received support from conservative and liberal politicians, academics, teachers, and powerful organizations on opposite sides of the wars.

However, "the needs of marginalized students [were never] the center of discussion in these very public arguments" (Martin, 2003, p. 11). Mathematics classrooms' potential to perpetuate social and racial stratification in America was not a battle that either side of the math wars was willing to fight. The math wars failed to acknowledge and account for, in meaningful ways, the extensive body of research on the crippling effects of systemic injustices (e.g., concentrated poverty, underfunded school districts) and negative cultural forces (e.g., racism, stereotypes) on students' academic performance.

In fact, a critical survey of the major trends and shifts that dominated the field in the twentieth century and that continue to shape twenty-first century classrooms shows that commitment to racial equity has been largely absent or at best shortsighted (Martin, 2003). Whether in the early decades of the twentieth century or during the 1960s resurgence of progressive tenets in education, "the more fundamental issue of power, of whose voice gets to be heard in determining what is best for poor children and children of color," never received adequate and critical attention (Delpit, 1988, p. 296). The "new math" movement brought more rigor to K-12 mathematics education and renewed efforts in repositioning and reaffirming America as the leader in scientific and technological innovations. But, there was nothing in the move-ment about the trend of Black Americans being "turned away" from mathe-matics and science education at an early age because of "tracking…poor access to the best-qualified teachers and inadequate resources" (McGee &

Martin, 2011, p. 48; Tate, 2000). From the 1970s "back-to-basics" uprising, the explosion of cognitive science in education, to the "math wars" punctuating the end of the century, the exclusion of generations of African Americans (and other racial minority groups) from STEM fields has never been appraised as a national crisis or emergency.

Instead, the ascension and vanishing of initiatives to reform mathematics education has, by and large, accepted and responded to the history of "under-achievement among underrepresented students...as the natural and normal starting point for research" and innovation in the field (Martin, 2003, p. 18). Equity, particularly as it pertains to race-based differences in academic attainments between Black students and their white and Asian counterparts, has never been central to mathematics education research.

Mathematics, its presumed acultural and apolitical nature, along with its universal body of knowledge, has survived the ebbs and flows of more than a century-old battle over content and pedagogy. However, a 100 years of fighting over what and how to teach in math classrooms have overshadowed a true account of one of the "real casualties" of the math wars:

> *It is a remarkable fact that research and policy orientations and conclusions pertaining to mathematics education for African American children have remained relatively unchanged. In particular, little progress has been made on the nature of the research questions that have been asked about these children, the kinds of conclusions that are generated about their skills and abilities, or the aims and goals for their mathematical education.*
>
> (Martin, 2009, p. 20)

The abundance of studies and data comparing the academic performance or attainments of racial groups – who is leading and who is lagging behind in the math ability pyramid – have maintained the perception and expectation of the mathematically "gifted" Asian and white male. They have created "an order of the world" of mathematics education, a reality that denies the "mathematical illiterates" – individuals who, like this study's participants, are stereotyped as mathematical failures – the critical space needed for reimagination or "to discover that these orders are perhaps not the only possible ones or the best ones" (Foucault, 1994, p. xx.)

Mathematics for All, or Some?

There have been attempts (e.g., NCTM, 1989, 2000) to integrate equity into mathematics education reform more meaningfully. However, those initiatives have assumed and adopted a conception of classrooms as spaces disconnected or shielded from social ills like unemployment, concentration of poverty, crime, racial, and social isolation. Such initiatives have based their recommendations on mathematics being ahistorical, universal, and "completely independent of culture" (Schoenfeld, 2004, p. 2).

The last few decades of the twentieth century saw mainstream reform movements challenge the ability or hierarchical model – only a few can and will succeed – that dominated and defined the field of mathematics since its inception. The National Council of Teachers of Mathematics (NCTM), founded in 1920 to counter progressive education's assault on mathematics, was one of the leading forces in propagating the idea of *Mathematics for All*. NCTM's (1989) *Curriculum and Evaluation Standards*, inspired ironically by many of the "themes of progressive education" from the 1920s, sent shock-waves through K-12 math education (Klein, 2003, p. 192). The nation's history of injustices perpetrated against women and people of color were highlighted as barriers to a more equitable educational landscape and to a more economically competitive US (NCTM, 1989, p. 4).

However, NCTM's call for equity and its standards did not include provisions on how to innovate math classrooms and curricula to address those injustices. The crippling impact of socioeconomic forces such as *multigenerational* poverty (Sharkey, 2013) on public schools' performance, students, and the overall communities those public institutions serve were not part of NCTM's agenda. For example, one of the recommendations was "technology-rich" classrooms for all. There was no consideration for chronic funding inequality and no mention of unequal access to technology – the *digital divide* which came into greater focus during COVID-19 – that, together, likely turned a push for more technology in math classrooms into the widening of existing "disparities…in class, gender, and race" (Apple, 1992, p. 417). NCTM's standards were founded on a "naïve assessment of the ways in which [America] produces inequalities" (p. 418). Efforts to pivot away from the hierarchical model to a more inclusive and egalitarian educational landscape were guided mostly by superficial and ahistorical assumptions about the existence and persistence of racial and gender-based inequalities in mathematics.

So, it is no surprise that, a decade after NCTM's (1989) call for more equity in mathematics education, America continued to trail many other advanced nations in mathematics and disparities between underserved students of color and their white counterparts persisted (Martin, 2003, pp. 8–9; see Lee, 2002; Schoenfeld, 2002).

As a response to the math wars, NCTM (2000) released a new set of standards. Equity is the first of NCTM's (2000) six principles, signaling a sense of urgency in the organization's fight against inequality in mathematics education. However, mentions of equity were dissociated from mathematics' history of excluding disproportionally more students of color and in low-income communities from economic opportunities (Martin, 2003, p. 9). *Mathematics for All* stressed the importance of culturally competent curricula and culturally responsive classrooms but oversimplified "the complexities of race and minority/marginalized status" that are salient in understanding and advancing theories about differences in students' academic performance (p. 10).

Deemphasizing racial injustice in efforts to innovate mathematics education so that it served the interests of (and appeared more inclusive to) 'all students' is not unique to the twentieth century or mathematics education. In many ways, it resembles recent efforts to undermine the *Black Lives Matter* movement with calls like "All Lives Matter" or "Blue Lives Matter" that, in the name of "inclusion" or "law and order," sought to deflect attention away from the country's anti-Blackness history and ongoing systems of oppression. NCTM's (2000) marginalization of racial inequality in its recommendations, in the name of "mathematics for all," stemmed from and continued a "long history" where the "needs and interests of Black children are in many ways dismissed" and deemed less important and always separate from the country's needs (Berry et al., 2013, p. 41; see also Martin, 2009). Racial inequality has been a fixture and uncontested reality in the field of mathematics education for decades. However, the field's noncommittal endorsement of equity and whitewashing of its role in widening race-based inequalities has allowed for "commonsense beliefs and official knowledge about who is competent (and not) in mathematics" to persist (McGee & Martin, 2011, p. 49).

Mathematics' rise to high-status discipline – a consequence of the rapid expansion of globalization and technology – has resulted in the exclusion of disproportionately more women and racial minorities from economic opportunities (e.g., Anyon, 1997; Connell, 1994; Noguera, 2003; Sharkey, 2013; Tate & Rousseau, 2002; Wilson, 2009). Yet, constructs like racism and race-based stereotypes continue to receive considerable less attention in mathematics educational research compared to studies on cognition or pedagogies (Lubienski, 2002; Lubienski & Bowen, 2000). NCTM's (1989, 2000) recommendations helped the field of mathematics education to adopt a more expansive and complex understanding of learning. Nonetheless, the failure to bridge the so-called race-based "gap" has allowed beliefs of a biological predisposition to succeed or fail in mathematics to persist. Essentialist explanations for why groups like African Americans do not succeed in mathematics at the same rate as their white or Asian counterparts have gained credence.

NEOLIBERAL ETHOS OF MATHEMATICS EDUCATION REFORM

Efforts to reform mathematics in the past century, though varied in substance and purpose, illustrate one of the fundamental flaws with the application of neoliberal or "liberal" ideals in public education. Liberalism, Esposito and Murphy (2010) argued, "it relies on presumably timeless, non-contingent standards to evaluate the adequacy of all persons, cultures, and institutions" (p. 42). Reforming the teaching and learning of mathematics, whether motivated by socioeconomic pressures or new discoveries in cognitive science, has always assumed and embraced and promoted "a world where [students] have the liberty to compete with others" and to use their experiences in math classrooms for "what will serve them best" (p. 42). Thus, explanations and understandings about "failure" to use mathematics as a pathway to better economic opportunities and greater social mobility have mostly – overtly or subliminally – focused on or presumed deficiencies in students, their communities, or their teachers. Consequently, efforts to unearth and combat racial inequality in the field have always been seen as fringe or somewhat radical. Studies, like this book, have failed to capture mainstream attention and continue to exist in the shadows of the field's central interests and concerns. Those efforts never seemed contiguous with the framing of math classrooms as necessary to maintain "capital[ism] and to continue US global dominance" (Gutstein, 2009, p. 138).

Mathematics education, its evolution from an elitist and exclusive enterprise to a necessary pillar for American democracy, has always espoused universal standards. The discipline's claim to neutrality and universality is rooted in

> ...*specific assumptions about human nature and social order that stifle diversity and support hierarchy. These background assumptions substantiate a type of racial and ethnic hegemony whereby the prevailing standards and norms that buttress white privilege (e.g., individualism, free competition, neutrality, etc.) are*

given an ahistorical status ... [and serve] to depoliticize and
ultimately legitimize racial and ethnic inequality.
                                    (Esposito & Murphy, 2010, p. 40)

Mathematics catapulted to the fore as part of a mid-twentieth century push to promote math (and science) classrooms as essential and foundational to the "American dream." Mathematics education became integral to marketing the country's capitalist system as "democratic" and meritocratic – success, the fruit of hard work and discipline, has been sold as being within everyone's reach. However, the reality has been and continues to be very different. Mathematics education, in K-12 and higher education, has more or less served as a ranking and filtering process – a process that has extinguished or derailed the dreams of generations of Americans.

Math classrooms are spaces where students, by high school, discover and learn to accept the "limits" of their academic or career prospects. Math scores have been used and continue to determine who "merits" access to richer and better resourced academic programs, scholarship funds, and more prestigious opportunities. And because of the discipline's assumed meritocratic and universal nature, the increased abstraction in mathematics instructions and assessments from K to 12, explicitly or subliminally, crystalizes for many, especially those who live in underserved communities and are enrolled in underresourced schools like Oxford, that there exists a hierarchy of academic ability.

Traditional mathematics education never allowed opportunities for students (and practitioners) to assess or challenge norms that directly and indirectly affect the learning and how it is done (e.g., primacy of algebra in K-12 curricula). Math curricula do not raise or invite questions about institutional "commonsense" policies and practices that have long been established as discriminatory (e.g., college placement exams; SATs):

...[f]amily income and parents' education, for example, are
correlated with SAT scores and also with college outcomes, so
that much of the apparent predictive power of the SAT actually
reflects the proxy effects of socioeconomic status.
                                    (Atkinson & Geiser, 2009, pp. 665–666)

On the contrary, those norms and policies have been normalized in mathematics education and in propagating beliefs about who can and cannot be a math person. They are an extension and serve as enforcement mechanisms of the neoliberal ethos – the timeless and universal "survival of the fittest" ethos – that underpinned the field of mathematics education.

In my view, if the field remains unwilling and uninterested in centering efforts on grappling with and reversing the discipline's history of racial and economic injustice, mathematics classrooms will continue to be a source and force for the proliferation and perpetuation of narratives about the intellectual and cultural inferiority of Black Americans.

IF NOT NOW, WHEN?

I have shown that calls to reform mathematics education, whether focused on pedagogy or based on broader curricular innovations, have failed to extend beyond traditional views of what it means to engage with mathematical content. It's also important to underscore that this view and tradition have always been reluctant and reticent to demonstrate or articulate a stance vis-à-vis existing injustices.

> *To the Mathematics Community, In light of the extrajudicial murders by police of George Floyd, Breonna Taylor, Tony McDade and numerous others before them, and the subsequent brutality of the police response to protests, we call on the mathematics community to boycott working with police departments. This is not an abstract call. Many of our colleagues can and do work with police departments to provide modeling and data work. Given the structural racism and brutality in US policing, we do not believe that mathematicians should be collaborating with police departments in this manner. It is simply too easy to create a "scientific" veneer for racism.*
>
> *(Aougab et al., 2020, p. 1293)*

The excerpt above is from an open letter, *Boycott Collaboration with police*, that was penned by a number of mathematicians in response to the recent public and televised murder of George Floyd by a Minneapolis police officer. This letter marked one of the few instances where the mathematics community acknowledged publicly their role in supporting and perpetuating racial injustices – here, in the form of police violence – in America. But, this letter is also an admission. It is a concession of the extraordinary circumstance, national, and international pressures needed to persuade mathematicians, the field of mathematics education, and researchers that they have been (and will likely continue to be) co-conspirators in maintaining this "scientific veneer for racism." The letter was reactive, and thus far, to my knowledge, mostly rhetorical in terms of the substantive and meaningful policy, scholarly, or pedagogical changes that it engendered or inspired.

So, the question remains: what will it take? Was the public lynching of George Floyd enough? Were the ensuing thousands of protests spanning across 60 countries, 7 continents, in the midst of the disproportionate impact of COVID-19 on the most vulnerable segments of our world population sufficient? Was any of it enough for the field of mathematics education to finally shift away from its neoliberal ideals and neutral bubble? Is it finally time for math classrooms to engage students in work that both affirms and supports their role and sense of belonging to the fight for a more just, humane, and equitable tomorrow (e.g., mathematics for social justice)?

The set of neoliberal assumptions that have governed the field's evolution this past century not only ignored the discipline's history of racial stratification and oppression but also exemplified the pernicious power of tradition and "scientific" knowledge and their foothold on social realities – America's anti-Black racist tradition, the high status, and presumed objectivity of mathematics combined to shield math classrooms from the 1960s' cataclysmic sociocultural reckoning. Mathematics has not only risen to a high-status discipline globally in the twentieth century, but also mathematical content and skills have gained more in importance and socioeconomic relevance, thus power, compared to other disciplines or disciplinary knowledge (e.g., Nielsen, 2003).

With the ubiquity of technology in all aspects of our lives, it is no surprise that the value of scientific or mathematical information has gained more control over both the type of knowledge generated and how it is generated. There is no debate about the need for research, practices, and training in most fields to be based on quantifiable, generalizable, reliable, and scientifically sound data collection processes. Nor is there any ambiguity about the seismic improvements in, for instance, global health outcomes and overall quality of life in the last few decades (e.g., Rosling, Rosling, & Rönnlund, 2018) because of knowledge generated through scientific experiments.

However, as was referenced in Aougab et al.'s (2020) open letter, mathematics and its applications do not exist and are not implemented in a vacuum or a just world. The creation and adoption of mathematical models and new technologies to fight crime is a perfect illustration of this. Those models and technologies (e.g., face recognition software) have been promoted and implemented as "colorblind," "morally superior" tools that are "above human bias" (Benjamin, 2019, p. 10). But, in fact, these tools have been blinded to the injustices of the American carceral system and its criminalization of Black bodies. The growing integration of those models in the American criminal system has ushered in a new era. One that Benjamin (2019) appropriately called the *New Jim Code*:

> *...in a recent audit of California's gang database, not only do Blacks and Latinxs constitute 87 percent of those listed, but [48] of the names turned out to be babies under the age of 1, some of whom were supposedly "self-described gang members."*
>
> (p. 6; see Harvey, 2016)

It's a new era, created by algorithms, automation, and machine learning, that is not only "structured by existing inequalities," but that also "codes" poor people of color and immigrants as "criminal...disposable, [and] unwanted" (p. 9).

Knowledge of mathematics presupposes learning as processes independent of and unaffected by larger sociopolitical and cultural forces. As such, mathematical knowledge, supposedly colorblind and "morally superior," dictates, controls, and reproduces a reality – one seldom questioned – that will always be unwilling and uninterested in disrupting existing inequity.

CONCLUSION

This chapter provided an overview of some of the major shifts in the field of mathematics education in the twentieth century. Emphasis was placed on the progressive movements of the early 1900s and the 1960s, the "new math" of the 1950s, and the "math wars" of a few decades later. I demonstrated how a hundred years of reform initiatives failed to integrate racial inequality into the conception and evolution of the field of mathematics education. A failure, if not addressed, will continue, well into the twenty-first century, to isolate, segregate, and code more generations of Americans out of the American dream.

Although this section did not attempt to historicize mathematics education, it made clear the field's history of abdicating responsibility and role in America's growing social inequalities. This chapter delineated some of the consequences of a high-status discipline's unwillingness to champion race-based equity as foundational to, and a constitutive aspect of what it means to teach, learn mathematics and produce scholarship.

One of those consequences is the fact that well-intentioned and competent teachers, such as Ms. Turner, are left with a specious assessment and distorted understanding of what it means to teach mathematics in underfunded urban public schools like Oxford and how to support students like this study's participants realize their full academic potential. Another is the fact that 11 highly motivated students could not find enough motivation, purpose, and reasons to pursue or even imagine the possibility of a STEM career through the "smog air," beyond the urban education tale and assumptions of a hierarchy of mathematics ability.

REFERENCES

Anyon, J. (1997). *Ghetto schooling: A political economy of urban educational reform.* New York, NY: Teachers College, Columbia University.

Aougab, T., Ardila, F., Athreya, J., Goins, E., Hoffman, C., Kent, A., ... Wehrheim, K. (2020). Boycott collaboration with police. *Notices of the American Mathematical Society, 67*(9), 1293–1294. Retrieved from https://www.ams.org/journals/notices/202009/rnoti-p1293.pdf

Apple, M. W. (1992). Do the Standards go far enough? *Journal for Research in Mathematics Education, 23,* 412–431.

Atkinson, R. C., & Geiser, S. (2009). Reflections on a century of college admissions tests. *Educational Researcher, 38*(9), 665–676. doi:10.3102/0013189X09351981

Benjamin, R. (2019). *Race after technology: Abolitionist tools for the new Jim code.* Cambridge: Polity Press.

Berry, R. Q., Pinter, H. H., & McClain, O. L. (2013). A critical review of K-12 mathematics education, 1900-present. In J. Leonard & D. B. Martin (Eds.), *The brilliance of black children in mathematics: Beyond the numbers and toward new discourse* (pp. 23–53). Charlotte, NC: Information Age Publishing.

Bonilla-Silva, E. (2001). *White supremacy and racism in the post-civil rights era.* Boulder, CO: Lynne Reinner.

Connell, R. W. (1994). Poverty and education. *Harvard Educational Review, 64*(2), 125–149.

Delpit, L. (1988). The silenced dialogue: Power and pedagogy in educating other people's children. *Harvard Educational Review, 58*(3), 280–298.

Esposito, L., & Murphy, J. W. (2010). Post civil rights racism and the need to challenge racial/ethnic inequality beyond the limits of liberalism. *Theory in Action, 3*(2), 38–63.

Foucault, M. (1994). *The order of things: An archaeology of the human sciences*. New York, NY: Vintage Books.

Gutstein, E. (2009). The politics of mathematics education in the US: Dominant and counter agendas. In B. Greer, S. Mukhopadhyay, A. B. Powell, & S. Nelson-Barber (Eds.), *Culturally responsive mathematics education* (pp. 137–164). New York, NY: Routledge.

Hall, S. (2008). Protest movements in the 1970s: The long 1960s. *Journal of Contemporary History, 43*(4), 655–672.

Harvey, A. (2016, September 27). The list that can take your life. *Huffington Post*. Retrieved from https://www.huffpost.com/entry/the-list-that-can-take-your-life_b_57eae82ce4b07f20daa0fd51

Herrera, T. A., & Owens, D. T. (2001). "The new new math?": Two reform movements in mathematics education. *Theory in Practice, 10*(2), 84–92.

Klein, D. (2003). A brief history of American K-12 mathematics education in the 20th century. In J. M. Royer (Ed.), *Mathematical cognition* (pp. 175–225). Greenwich, CT: Information Age Publishing.

Lee, J. (2002). Racial and ethnic achievement gap trends: Reversing the progress toward equity? *Educational Researcher, 31*(1), 3–12.

Lubienski, S. T. (2002). A closer look at black-white mathematics gaps: Intersections of race and SES in NAEP achievement and instructional practices data. *The Journal of Negro Education, 71*(4), 269–287.

Lubienski, S. T., & Bowen, A. (2000). Who's counting? A survey of mathematics education research 1982–1998. *Journal for Research in Mathematics Education, 31*(5), 626–633.

Martin, D. B. (2003). Hidden assumptions and unaddressed questions in *mathematics for all* in rhetoric. *The Mathematics Educator, 13*(2), 7–21.

Martin, D. (2009). *Mathematics teaching, learning, and liberation in the lives of black children*. Abingdon: Routledge.

Martin, D. B. (2012). Learning mathematics while Black. *The Journal of Educational Foundations, 26*, 47–66.

McGee, E., & Martin, D. (2011). From the hood to being hooded: A case study of a Black male PhD. *Journal of African American Males, 2,* 46–65.

National Commission on Excellence in Education. (1983). A nation at risk: The imperative for educational reform. *The Elementary School Journal, 84*(2), 112–130.

National Council of Teachers of Mathematics. (1989). *Curriculum and evaluation standards for school mathematics.* Reston, VA: Author.

National Council of Teachers of Mathematics. (2000). *Principles and standards for school mathematics.* Reston, VA: Author.

Nielsen, R. H. (2003). How to do educational research in university mathematics? *The Mathematics Educator, 13,* 33–40. Retrieved from http://math.coe.uga.edu/tme/Issues/v13n1/v13n1.Nielsen.pdf

Noguera, P. A. (2003). *City schools and the American dream: Reclaiming the promise of public education.* New York, NY: Teachers College Press.

Rosling, H., Rosling, O., & Rönnlund, A. R. (2018). *Factfulness: Ten reasons we're wrong about the world - And why things are better than you think* (1st ed.). New York, NY: Flatiron Books.

Rury, J. L., & Hill, S. (2013). An end of innocence: African-American high school protest in the 1960s and 1970s. *History of Education, 42*(4), 486–508.

Schoenfeld, A. H. (2002). Making mathematics work for all children: Issues of standards, testing, and equity. *Educational Researcher, 31*(1), 13–25.

Schoenfeld, A. H. (2004). The math wars. *Educational Policy, 18,* 253–286.

Schoenfeld, A. H. (2016). Research in mathematics education. *Review of Research in Education, 40,* 497–528.

Sharkey, P. (2013). *Stuck in place: Urban neighborhoods and the end of progress toward racial equality.* Chicago, IL: The University of Chicago Press.

Sheffield, L. J. (2017). Dangerous myths about "gifted" students. *Journal of ZDM Mathematics Education, 49,* 13–23.

Tate, W. F. (1997). Race, ethnicity, SES, gender, and language proficiency trends in mathematics achievement: An update. *Journal for Research in Mathematics Education, 28*(6), 652–680.

Tate, W. F. (2000). Summary: Some final thoughts on changing the faces of mathematics. In W. G. Secada (Ed.), *Changing the faces of mathematics: Perspectives on African Americans* (pp. 201–207). Reston, VA: NCTM.

Tate, W. F., & Rousseau, C. (2002). Access and opportunity: The political and social context of mathematics education. In L. English (Ed.), *International handbook of research in mathematics education* (pp. 271–300). Mahwah, NJ: Erlbaum.

Usiskin, Z. (1985). We need another revolution in secondary school mathematics. In C. Hirsch & M. Zweng (Eds.), *The secondary school mathematics curriculum* (pp. 1–21). Reston, VA: National Council of Teachers of Mathematics.

Walker, F. N. (2012). *Building mathematics learning communities: Improving outcomes in urban high schools.* New York, NY: Teachers College Press.

Wilson, W. J. (2009). The political and economic forces shaping concentrated poverty. *Political Science Quarterly, 123*(4), 555–571.

7

CONCLUSION

Identity, framed here as multilayered social and cultural processes, began to interest educational researchers and other fields of study – outside of psychology – around the middle of the twentieth century (Appiah, 2018, p. 3). For this book, the multidimensional and complex nature of identity elicited considerations that extend beyond the field of mathematics education.

Aspects of the historical, schooling, disciplinary, and classroom contexts in which students developed their relationships to mathematics helped to ground and shape the analyses and arguments delineated here. These layers, individually and collectively, spotlighted the pervasiveness and depths of institutional racism in mathematics education. They provided much needed insights into how 11 Black and Brown students evaluated their classroom experiences in relationship to what W. E. B. Du Bois (1903/1996) called the veil:

> *...this sense of always looking at one's self through the eyes of others, of measuring one's soul by the tape of a world that looks on in an amused contempt and pity.*
>
> *(p. 5)*

LIMITATIONS

As stated earlier, this study was part of an ongoing, larger college pipeline program and research project sponsored by the firm E&Y and carried out by the Cecil B. Moore University. Students received a better supported and more rigorous mathematics education compared to other Oxford seniors. This is one possible limitation of this study: the heightened level of rigor and abstraction could have widened the gap that some participants believed existed between their academic abilities and what is required to be a math person. For example, being part of the college pipeline program somewhat discouraged Kendrick and Tyronne, both considered "example kids" in earlier grades, to conceive of college level mathematics as a possibility. The level of sophistication solidified many students' convictions that the label math person, particularly as it relates to a college major or career path, should be reserved for others.

Another potential limitation for this ethnographic study is my own experiences as a mathematics educator and researcher. I have learned to expect and accept people's disbelief or surprise as a response to my teaching college math. I am unsure of the cumulative impact of those moments on my own (emerging) identity as a researcher or college professor. However, I am confident that they played a role. The regularity – and really inevitability – of those moments likely factored in my decision to study an honor's precalculus classroom of predominantly Black students from a low-income community in northeast Philadelphia. Those moments surely contributed to my defining and framing of math identity as a story of belonging – a story that "was as much about [students] and their narration of their experiences [in mathematics education] as it was my own" (Ibrahim, 1999, p. 355). Thus, my interactions with students, my observations, and my analyses of their relationship with mathematics were colored, and perhaps driven, by this search for coherence and substance for something different, a counter to the narrative of failure typically associated with Black students.

Another limitation of this project is its potential to be misinterpreted or misread as presenting an argument for all Black students. This study subscribed to the qualitative paradigm and made use of ethnographic methods to collect and analyze data. Qualitative studies, being descriptive in nature, require very detailed (thick) narrative description of a phenomenon – in this case racial inequality in mathematics education – through the eyes of a relatively small group of participants. The data used and analyzed here are about 11 students. Patterns found and analyses developed in this book cannot be generalized to all students of color or Black American teenagers in K-12 mathematics education – this would be a continuation or rebranding of the urban education tale, another master narrative about what Black kids living in low-income communities lack or cannot do.

This book seeks to shed a spotlight on racism in the teaching and learning of mathematics. It does not intend to propagate existing disparaging views of people of color. Students' struggle to develop a sense of belonging to the exclusive community of "geniuses" is an indictment of the field of mathematics education, an account of widening educational inequalities in the United States, and a reminder of the pernicious effects of systemic racism. It is not evidence or ammunition for race-based beliefs of who can or cannot be a math person. On the contrary, the 11 stories in this book provide researchers, practitioners, and students new ways to discuss and think about racial inequality in mathematics. Participants' stories and voices invite us all to look beyond the "veil" and to give serious considerations to "the identity work that students do in conjunction with learning the content of a discipline" (Valeras, Martin, & Kane, 2012, p. 336).

This book joins others in calling for greater investment in ways to create and support belonging for students in the face of disciplinary gatekeeping practices and in spite of a tradition rooted in racist and sexist ideologies.

BEYOND THE "VEIL"

This book echoes other scholars' call for new policy and curricular initiatives aimed at challenging the underrepresentation of Black students in STEM fields (e.g., Lee, 2002; Schoenfeld, 2002; Tate, 1997). Students from low-income communities, like this study's participants, often exhibit greater difficulty "setting their reality aside to engage in mathematics classroom investigations that do not connect to their reality" (McNair, 2000, p. 559; see also Bruckerhoff, 1995). Thus, math classrooms that require students, particularly those living in communities still reeling from racist policies from the past century, to set their realities aside as a precondition for success are likely to perpetuate the so-called race-based achievement gap. They will likely continue to legitimate beliefs of a racial hierarchy of math ability. Disrupting this cycle means more studies and professional development opportunities on ways to connect mathematics to students' everyday lives.

There have been attempts to address mathematics classrooms' potential to exacerbate racial inequality. One recent example is *mathematics for social justice* (e.g., Esmonde, 2014; Gutstein & Peterson, 2013). The idea is to use mathematics classrooms and content as spaces where students can develop better understanding of "relations of power, resource inequities, and disparate opportunities between social groups" (Gutstein, 2006, p. 335). Acknowledging and abandoning the discipline's history of exclusion asks that we provide students with

> ...*sociopolitical consciousness of the conditions of their lives, communities,' and broader society/world (reading the world); a sense of social agency, or a belief that they are capable of acting on the world to affect change toward social justice (writing the*

world); and positive cultural/ social identities – that is, to be strongly rooted in their language(s), culture(s), and community and have the confidence to stand up for, and act on, what they believe.

(Gutstein, 2006, p. 332)

For example, nearly half of American college students are placed in "developmental math" or/and in other pre-college level courses (Parker, Traver, & Cornick, 2018, p. 25; see Bailey & Jaggars, 2016). Unsurprisingly, and because of this country's racist history and growing educational inequalities in the United States, this phenomenon has had an outsized impact on students of color. Developmental math courses, designed to provide students skills and tools needed to succeed in college, have been found to further disadvantage "Black students" who are among college students "less likely ... to complete their developmental coursework" (p. 26). Being placed in these courses send an unambiguous message to students: "you are not college material." In essence, these pre-college courses continue mathematics education's history of exclusion; they are keeping alive the perception of a racial pyramid of academic potential or ability.

Reversing this trend requires learning experiences that go beyond the common use of "applications" or "real-life" examples (e.g., pizza as application for fractions; filling up a pool as application for constant rate of change) in the teaching and learning of mathematics. K-12 and college mathematics classrooms need to help students realize – and perhaps initiate actions to disrupt the fact – that their mathematics college placement is more likely a result of socioeconomic injustice and educational inequity than it is a reflection of their academic abilities or professional prospects.

Another example of reconceptualizing mathematics curricula and instructions to address the discipline's oppressive history is Robert Moses' *Algebra Project*. Founded in the 1980s, the project's main concern was with "the mathematical and scientific literacy requirements that [were] becoming prerequisites both for citizenship and for competing in the emerging global economy" (Silva, Moses, Rivers, & Johnson, 1990, p. 378). The project, and its focus on mathematics literacy, rejected the perception of mathematics education as a neutral or value-free academic enterprise. In fact, it shared some of the central tenets of mathematics for social justice and advocated for learning that is "grounded in an acknowledgment of the social construction of mathematics" (p. 383).

However, attempts like the ones mentioned above need greater governmental, public support, and endorsement from the larger mathematics community if they are ever to effect meaningful and enduring social changes.

Unlike the field's embrace and implementation of many of NCTM's (1989, 2000) recommendations, mathematics education has mostly steered clear of initiatives like the Algebra Project. It has not integrated or invested in movements like mathematics for social justice as part of the field's fight against racial disparities – some of the explanations for this are detailed in the previous chapter. This is one of the reasons that some have characterized the field's calls for racial equity as empty rhetoric (Martin, 2003) and still a manifestation of looking at racial inequality through the "veil."

The reconceptualization of math instructions and curricula should also be coupled with more efforts from policymakers and institutions to eradicate "color blindness" out of teacher education programs and professional developments (Gay, 2002). Colorblind assumptions are more prevalent in mathematics and science education. Their potential adverse effects on students are compounded by the fact that only 18% of the teaching workforce are people of color (Boser, 2014, p. 2). Rousseau and Tate's (2003) study of a group of mathematics teachers' reflections on equity found that white teachers were more likely to adopt color blindness out of fear of stereotyping Black and Brown students. In those teachers' view, mentions of racial differences (i.e., acknowledging racism) were synonymous to harboring racist sentiments toward students (pp. 213–214). A teaching workforce overwhelmingly white and where the average teacher is pedagogically unprepared and ideologically unmotivated – in some cases, opposed – to creating learning experiences for more students of color to develop positive math identities represents another significant barrier to bridging the race-based opportunity gap.

This book provides a deeper and more nuanced understanding of math identity in relationship to mainstream race-based beliefs that pervade education. It also underscores a need to go beyond the veil. If the field of mathematics is ever to truly embrace racial equity as a core and guiding principle, it needs to fundamentally and categorically reject the idea of "math genes." It needs to depart from the ability model and to wage "war" on other exclusionary assumptions that have long underpinned and guided what we, as a society, have come to accept as the teaching and learning of mathematics.

MATH WARS ON RACIAL INEQUALITY

This book is also a call for a new social imaginary. One in which Black, Indigenous, and People of Color "are not born in exile" and no longer need to

> endure a thousand cuts and slashes that wound their spirits and
> require [them] to engage in daily triage to protect their souls. A new

America, no longer tethered to the value gap, would make it possible for millions of Black people...to finally [belong] without...that unsettling feeling of being "in but not of."

(Glaude, 2020, p. 212)

Glaude's (2020) critically acclaimed book *Begin Again* cautioned that if this nation ever wishes to be a true democratic and multicultural society, it will need to renounce the *lie* and severe ties with the *value gap* – the idea that white lives matter more. An idea and a "lie" that has informed, structured, and guided our institutions, policies, history, and national identity. A lie that has "allowed America to [continually] avoid the truth about its unjust treatment of black people" (p. 8).

The value gap has allowed racial inequality in mathematics education to become an accepted and expected reality. The lie has allowed more than a century of reform initiatives to skirt around or avoid confronting the discipline's past and continuing contributions to racial injustice. It has freed the mathematics community from ever seeing the need for, and value in, committing to an antiracist agenda – racial inequality is not a math problem.

My hope is that this book and these 11 students' stories make clear that it's time for new "math wars," this time, centered on and unapologetic about eradicating racial inequality in mathematics education.

REFERENCES

Appiah, K. A. (2018). *The lies that bind: Rethinking identity, creed, country, color.* New York, NY: W. W. Norton & Company.

Bailey, T., & Jaggars, S. S. (2016, June 2). *When college students start behind.* The Century Foundation. Retrieved from https://tcf.org/content/report/college-students-start-behind/

Boser, U. (2014). *Teacher diversity revisited: A new state-by-state analysis.* Washington, DC: Center for American Progress. Retrieved from https://www.americanprogress.org/issues/race/reports/2014/05/04/88962/teacher-diversity-revisited/

Bruckerhoff, C. (1995). Life in the bricks. *Urban Education, 30*(3), 317–336.

Du Bois, W. E. B. (1903/1996). *Souls of black folk.* New York, NY: Penguin Books.

Esmonde, I. (2014). "Nobody's rich and nobody's poor ... It sounds good, but it's actually not": Affluent students learning mathematics and social justice. *Journal of the Learning Sciences*, 23(3), 348–391. doi:10.1080/10508406.2013.847371

Gay, G. (2002). Preparing for culturally responsive teaching. *Journal of Teacher Education*, 53(2), 106–116.

Glaude, E. S. (2020). *Begin again: James Baldwin's America and its urgent lessons for our own*. New York, NY: Crown.

Gutstein, E. (2006). "The real world as we have seen it": Latino/a parents voice on teaching mathematics for social justice. *Mathematical Thinking and Learning*, 8(3), 331–358.

Gutstein, E., & Peterson, B. (2013). *Rethinking mathematics: Teaching social justice by the numbers*. Milwaukee, WI: Rethinking Schools.

Ibrahim, A. F. K. M. (1999). Becoming black: Rap and hip hop, race, gender, identity, and the politics of ESL learning. *TESOL Quarterly*, 33(3), 349–369.

Lee, O. (2002). Science inquiry for elementary students from diverse backgrounds. In W. G. Secada (Ed.), *Review of research in education* (Vol. 26, pp. 23–69). Washington, DC: American Educational Research Association.

Martin, D. B. (2003). Hidden assumptions and unaddressed questions in *mathematics for all* in rhetoric. *The Mathematics Educator*, 13(2), 7–21.

McNair, R. E. (2000). Life outside of mathematics classroom: Implications for mathematics reform. *Urban Education*, 34(5), 550–570.

National Council of Teachers of Mathematics. (1989). *Curriculum and evaluation standards for school mathematics*. Reston, VA: Author.

National Council of Teachers of Mathematics. (2000). *Principles and standards for school mathematics*. Reston, VA: Author.

Parker, S., Traver, A., & Cornick, J. (2018). Contextualizing developmental math content into introduction to sociology in community colleges. *Teaching Sociology*, 46(1), 25–33. Retrieved from http://www.jstor.org/stable/26429254

Rousseau, C., & Tate, W. (2003). No time like the present: Reflecting on equity in school mathematics. *Theory Into Practice*, 42(3), 210–216. Retrieved from http://www.jstor.org/stable/1477422

Schoenfeld, A. H. (2002). Making mathematics work for all children: Issues of standards, testing, and equity. *Educational Researcher, 31*(1), 13–25.

Silva, C. M., Moses, R. P., Rivers, J., & Johnson, P. (1990). The Algebra project: Making middle school mathematics count. *The Journal of Negro Education, 59*(3), 375–391.

Tate, W. F. (1997). Race-ethnicity, SES, gender, and language proficiency trends in mathematics achievement: An update. *Journal for Research in Mathematics Education, 28*(6), 652–679.

Valeras, M., Martin, D. B., & Kane, J. M. (2012). Content learning and identity construction: A framework to strengthen African American students' mathematics and science learning in urban elementary schools. *Human Development, 55*, 319–339.

APPENDICES

APPENDIX A: SURVEY ON MATHEMATICS CONFIDENCE

Name: _____   Date:_____

1: Confident   2: Somewhat Confident   3: A little Confident   4: Not Confident

#	Questions	1	2	3	4
1	I understand the math that I'm doing in this course.				
2	I will do well in this course.				
3	I am ready for more difficult college math courses				
4	I can do well in majors that require advanced math courses.				
5	I will pursue careers that involve knowing and using some advanced math concepts.				
6	I will likely go into careers that require a lot of college mathematics				
7	Mathematics is one of my favorite subjects.				
8	I will use mathematics outside of the classroom				
9	I'm a part of the learners and doers of the mathematics community.				
10	Mathematics will play some role in my future.				

APPENDIX B: PROTOCOL ON ACCUMULATED EXPERIENCES IN MATH

(1) What is your general feeling about mathematics? Can you explain what you mean?

(2) How has your experience in mathematics classrooms been? Can you give an example?

(3) Do you think that there's such a thing as a math person? How would you define a math person? Or what does a math person look like to you? Can you give an example?

(4) Are you a math person? Why or why not?

(5) Were you ever a math person? How did you figure out that you were or were not a math person?

(6) Do you have any friends in/out of school that are math people? Can you explain why you think that?

(7) Do you have any family members that are math people? Can you explain why you think that?

(8) Can you think of a time or moments in your life where you felt like you were a math person?

(9) Can you think of a time or moments in your life where you felt like you were not a math person?

(10) How important is math to you? How important is math to the kind of life you want to have?

APPENDIX C: PROTOCOL ABOUT STUDENTS' MATH CONFIDENCE

(1) How would you rate your overall confidence in math (from 1 to 10 or high, medium or low)? What is the meaning of that rating?

(2) What would you say is the number one reason for your level of confidence in mathematics? Can you explain why?

(3) What do you think it means to learn mathematics? How much of this do you think is the reason for your level of confidence in mathematics? Explain.

(4) Some researchers in the field define math confidence as "a sense of belongingness" to the community of math learners and doers. What does this mean to you?

(5) Do you feel like you belong to the community of math learners and doers? Why do you think that is? Can you give an example?

(6) When did you realize that you were/were not a member of the math community? Can you explain what specifically happened? Or can you describe that moment?

(7) How much of your sense of belonging/not belonging to the math community do you think contributes to the amount of effort that you usually put into your math classes?

(8)   Being a member of a racial minority group often means being sub-
       jected to various negative racial characterizations. In math, for
       instance, there is this perception that Asians and whites are better in
       math than Blacks. Are you aware of this? When or how would you
       say you became aware of this?
(9)   Do you think it easier or harder for Black students to feel that they
       belong to the community of math learners/doers? Can you explain
       what you mean?
(10)   What does it mean to be Black to you? Can you explain?
(11)   Have you ever thought of the kind of impact that being Black has
       on your sense of belonging/not belonging to the math community of
       learners? If not, then what kind of impact do you think that being
       Black has on a student's sense of belonging to the math community
       of learners? Can you explain?
(12)   What are some things that these questions made you think/talk about
       that you never had to before?
(13)   What is a question that you'd like to ask me?

APPENDIX D: INFORMED CONSENT   ASSENT FOR PARTICIPANTS UNDER 18

Dear Student,

Congratulations on your acceptance into the College Pathways program at
Frankford High School. Your success in college depends on how well prepared
you are to meet the academic and emotional challenges you will face there.
This year you will be taking courses in English and Math that have been
designed to help prepare you for such challenges.

As members of Temple University's College of Education who are involved
with this program, we're conducting research to help discover whether our
efforts to prepare you for college are successful. We're writing to ask your
permission to participate in this research. Throughout the school year, you'll
be doing assignments and participating in activities as part of this program. If
you'd like to contribute to the research, some of the things you do for class will
be collected and used in the study. Additionally, you may be asked to talk with
a member of the research team about your experiences with specific assignments and activities throughout the school year. These conversations will be
audio recorded.

The title of the study is: Preparing students for college: Examining the
effectiveness of a College Pathways program. The researchers involved are
Professors Michael W. Smith and Kristie Jones Newton, and doctoral students
Jon-Philip Imbrenda and Thierry Saintine, all from College of Education.

Here are some things you should know about the research study:

- Someone will explain this research study to you.
- You volunteer to be part of the study.
- Whether you take part is up to you.
- You can choose not to take part in the research study, in which case your work will not be included.
- You can agree to take part now and later change your mind.
- Whatever you decide, it will not be held against you.
- Feel free to ask all the questions you want before and after you decide.
- *By signing this consent form, you are not waiving any of the legal rights that you otherwise would have as a participant in a research study.*

The estimated duration of your study participation is September 1, 2015 to June 15, 2016.

The study will involve the following things. All of these are part of your regular classroom learning.

- You will be tested at the beginning and end of the school year to assess your reading, writing, and problem-solving.
- Your class and homework assignments will be collected throughout the school year.
- A member of the research team may ask to talk with you individually about specific assignments.
- You may be asked to talk aloud while you work on a reading assignment or mathematics problem in the presence of a member of the research team.
- At the beginning and end of the school year, you will complete a brief survey in which you describe your study habits and attitudes toward school.

The benefit you will obtain from the research is knowing that you have added to the understanding of this topic, and you will benefit from additional teachers and instruction tailored to your specific goals.

If you choose not to participate, you'll still be doing the same classwork. We just won't be using your words when we report the results. Please contact the research team with questions, concerns, or complaints about the research and any research-related injuries by calling 856-366-9812, or by emailing Jon-Philip Imbrenda at jay.imbrenda@temple.edu; or calling 212-283-6802 or emailing Thierry Saintine at thierry.saintine@temple.edu.

This research has been reviewed and approved by the Temple University Institutional Review Board. Please contact them at (215) 707-3390 or email them at: irb@temple.edu for any of the following: questions, concerns, or complaints about the research; questions about your rights; to obtain information; or to offer input.

Confidentiality: Efforts will be made to limit the disclosure of your personal information, including research study records, to people who have a need to review this information. However, the study team cannot promise complete secrecy. For example, although the study team has put in safeguards to protect your information, there is always a potential risk of loss of confidentiality. There are several organizations that may inspect and copy your information to make sure that the study team is following the rules and regulations regarding research and the protection of human subjects. These organizations include the IRB, Temple University, its affiliates and agents, Temple University Health System, Inc., its affiliates and agents, the study sponsor and its agents, and the Office for Human Research Protections.

Your name will never be used in reporting the results of this study.

Your Signature Documents your Permission to Take Part in this Research.

DO NOT SIGN THIS FORM AFTER THIS DATE →

_____
Signature of subject   Date

_____
Printed name of subject

_____
Signature of person obtaining consent

_____
Printed name of person obtaining consent

_____
Signature of witness (required)

_____
Printed name of witness (required)

Because the research requires recording your voice, please indicate if you are willing to be audiotaped by checking either Yes or No below.

I give my permission for these tapes to be used from: *September 1, 2015 to completion of the study.*

Data will be stored for three (3) years after completion of the study.

I understand that I can withdraw my permission at any time. Upon my request, the audiotape(s) will no longer be used.

Yes _____ No_____

APPENDIX E: INFORMED CONSENT – PARENT PERMISSION FORM

Dear Parent or Guardian,

In collaboration with Temple University, Frankford High School is offering a program to help prepare students for success in college. The program will take place in specially designed English and Math courses. Your child has been selected for these courses. Congratulations on this wonderful opportunity.

As members of Temple's College of Education who are involved in this program, we're writing to ask your permission to include your child in a study. The study will help to determine how successful we are in meeting our goal of preparing your child for college. If your child participates, work that he or she completes throughout the school year, as well as spoken accounts of his or her experiences in the program, may be included in the study. These conversations will be audio recorded.

The title of the study is: Preparing students for college: Examining the effectiveness of a College Pathways program. The researchers involved are Professors Michael W. Smith and Kristie Jones Newton, and doctoral students Jon-Philip Imbrenda and Thierry Saintine, all from the College of Education.

Here are some things you should know about the research study:

- Someone will explain this research study to your child.
- Your child can volunteer to be in a research study.
- Whether your child takes part is up to you.
- Your child can choose not to take part in the research study, in which case his or her work will not be included.
- Your child can agree to take part now and later change his or her mind.
- Whatever you decide, it will not be held against you.
- Feel free to ask all the questions you want before and after you decide.
- *By signing this consent form, you are not waiving any of the legal rights that your child otherwise would have as a participant in a research study.*

The estimated time in which your child will participate is September 1, 2015 to June 15, 2016.

The study will include the following things, all of which are part of regular classroom activity:

- Your child will be assessed at the beginning and end of the school year on reading, writing, and problem-solving.

- Your child's class and homework assignments will be collected throughout the school year.
- Your child may be asked to talk with a member of the research team about his or her experiences with specific assignments.
- Your child may be asked to talk aloud while working on a reading assignment or mathematics problem in the presence of a member of the research team.
- Your child will complete a brief survey at the beginning and end of the school year to help describe his or her study skills and attitudes toward schooling.

The benefit you will obtain from the research is knowing that you have contributed to the understanding of this topic, and your child will benefit from the involvement of additional teachers as well as instruction tailored to his or her individual needs. If you choose not to have your child participate, he or she will still be doing the same work. We just won't be using your child's words when we report the results.

Please contact the research team with questions, concerns, or complaints about the research and any research-related injuries by calling 856-366-9812 or emailing Jon-Philip Imbrenda at jay.imbrenda@temple.edu; or calling or calling 212-283-6802 or emailing Thierry Saintine at thierry.saintine@temple.edu.

This research has been reviewed and approved by the Temple University Institutional Review Board. Please contact them at (215) 707-3390 or email them at: irb@temple.edu for any of the following: questions, concerns, or complaints about the research; questions about your rights; to obtain information; or to offer input.

Confidentiality: Efforts will be made to limit the disclosure of your personal information, including research study records, to people who have a need to review this information. However, the study team cannot promise complete secrecy. For example, although the study team has put in safeguards to protect your information, there is always a potential risk of loss of confidentiality. There are several organizations that may inspect and copy your information to make sure that the study team is following the rules and regulations regarding research and the protection of human subjects. These organizations include the IRB, Temple University, its affiliates and agents, Temple University Health System, Inc., its affiliates and agents, the study sponsor and its agents, and the Office for Human Research Protections.

Your child's name will never be used in reporting the results of this study.

Signature Block for Children

Your Signature Documents your Permission for the Named Child to Take Part in this Research.

DO NOT SIGN THIS FORM AFTER THIS DATE →

_____
Printed name of child

_____   _____
Signature of parent or guardian   Date

_____   ❑ Parent
Printed name of parent or guardian   ❑ Guardian

                                                                              _____

_____   _____
Signature of person obtaining consent and assent   Date

_____   _____
Printed name of person obtaining consent and assent   Date

Because the research requires recording your child's voice, please indicate if you are willing to allow your child to be audiotaped by checking Yes or No below.

I give my permission for these tapes to be used from: _September 1, 2015 to completion of the study._

Data will be stored for three (3) years after completion of the study.

I understand that I can withdraw my permission at any time. Upon my request, the audiotape(s) will no longer be used.

Yes _____ No _____

APPENDIX F: INFORMED CONSENT – ASSENT FOR PARTICIPANTS 18 OR OLDER

Dear Student,

Congratulations on your acceptance into the College Pathways program at Frankford High School. Your success in college depends on how well prepared you are to meet the academic and emotional challenges you will face there. This year you will be taking courses in English and Math that have been designed to help prepare you for such challenges.

As members of Temple University's College of Education who are involved with this program, we're conducting research to help discover whether our efforts to prepare you for college are successful. We're writing to ask your permission to participate in this research. Throughout the school year, you'll be doing assignments and participating in activities as part of this program. If you'd like to contribute to the research, some of the things you do for class will be collected and used in the study. Additionally, you may be asked to talk with a member of the research team about your experiences with specific assignments and activities throughout the school year. These conversations will be audio recorded.

The title of the study is: Preparing students for college: Examining the effectiveness of a College Pathways program. The researchers involved are Professors Michael W. Smith and Kristie Jones Newton, and doctoral students Jon-Philip Imbrenda and Thierry Saintine, all from College of Education.

Here are some things you should know about the research study:

- Someone will explain this research study to you.
- You volunteer to be part of the study.
- Whether you take part is up to you.
- You can choose not to take part in the research study, in which case your work will not be included.
- You can agree to take part now and later change your mind.
- Whatever you decide, it will not be held against you.
- Feel free to ask all the questions you want before and after you decide.
- *By signing this consent form, you are not waiving any of the legal rights that you otherwise would have as a participant in a research study.*

The estimated duration of your study participation is from September 1, 2015 to June 15, 2016.

The study will involve the following things. All of these are part of your regular classroom learning.

- You will be tested at the beginning and end of the school year to assess your reading, writing, and problem solving.
- Your class and homework assignments will be collected throughout the school year.
- A member of the research team may ask to talk with you individually about specific assignments.
- You may be asked to talk aloud while you work on a reading assignment or mathematics problem in the presence of a member of the research team.
- At the beginning and end of the school year, you will complete a brief survey in which you describe your study habits and attitudes toward school.

The benefit you will obtain from the research is knowing that you have added to the understanding of this topic, and you will benefit from additional teachers and instruction tailored to your specific goals.

If you choose not to participate, you'll still be doing the same classwork. We just won't be using your words when we report the results. Please contact the research team with questions, concerns, or complaints about the research and any research-related injuries by calling 856-366-9812, or by emailing Jon-Philip Imbrenda at jay.imbrenda@temple.edu; or calling 212-283-6802 or emailing Thierry Saintine at thierry.saintine@temple.edu.

This research has been reviewed and approved by the Temple University Institutional Review Board. Please contact them at (215) 707-3390 or e-mail them at: irb@temple.edu for any of the following: questions, concerns, or complaints about the research; questions about your rights; to obtain information; or to offer input.

Confidentiality: Efforts will be made to limit the disclosure of your personal information, including research study records, to people who have a need to review this information. However, the study team cannot promise complete secrecy. For example, although the study team has put in safeguards to protect your information, there is always a potential risk of loss of confidentiality. There are several organizations that may inspect and copy your information to make sure that the study team is following the rules and regulations regarding research and the protection of human subjects. These organizations include the IRB, Temple University, its affiliates and agents, Temple University Health System, Inc., its affiliates and agents, the study sponsor and its agents, and the Office for Human Research Protections.

Your name will never be used in reporting the results of this study.

Your Signature Documents your Permission to Take Part in this Research.

DO NOT SIGN THIS FORM AFTER THIS DATE →

_____   _____
Signature of subject   Date

_____
Printed name of subject

_____
Signature of person obtaining consent

_____
Printed name of person obtaining consent

_____
Signature of witness (required)

_____
Printed name of witness (required)

Because the research requires recording your voice, please indicate if you are willing to be audiotaped by checking either Yes or No below.

I give my permission for these tapes to be used from: *September 1, 2015 to completion of the study.*

Data will be stored for three (3) years after completion of the study.

I understand that I can withdraw my permission at any time. Upon my request, the audiotape(s) will no longer be used.

Yes _____ No_____

APPENDIX G: LEVELS OF ANALYSES AND CODING

Stage I – Codes from Field Notes	Stage II – Codes after First Round of Interviews	Stage III – Codes after Second Round of Interviews	Stage IV – Codes after Triangulating Multiple Data Sources and Using Dedoose's "Data Analysis" Feature

• Teacher preparation (Ms. Turner's disinterest in planning; her reliance on tricks; her lack of focus during meetings)
• Students' engagement level (students' lack of interest in the course)
• Oxford's culture vs. Classroom culture
• Ms. Turner's beliefs about students' ability
• Ms. Turner's views of students' backgrounds
	• Overall math experience (mostly positive in elementary/ middle school; secondary math education; avoid higher level math)
	• Positive experiences
	• Negative experiences
	• Avoidance
	• Attitude
	• Achievement paradox (students wanted good grades and were always checking their grades; they were not as
		• Overall math confidence
		• Students' perception of a math person
		• Students' inability to view classmates as math people
		• Stereotypes – Asians and whites are smarter than Blacks
		• Racial identity (being Black means better than average)
		• The classroom as opportunity
			(1) Math experiences
			  • Mostly positive
			  • Experiences used to delegitimize performance in honor's precalculus
			(2) A math person
			  • Predisposed to succeed in math
			  • Knows the rules
			  • Good with money
			  • A great thinker
			(3) Math confidence
			  • Discrepancy in confidence level scores

(Continued)

Stage I – Codes from Field Notes	Stage II – Codes after First Round of Interviews	Stage III – Codes after Second Round of Interviews	Stage IV – Codes after Triangulating Multiple Data Sources and Using Dedoose's "Data Analysis" Feature
• Ms. Turner's beliefs about teaching math • Security officers (their interactions with students) • Nigel – the star, "overconfident" student-athlete • Kawhi – the quiet, high-ability student • Tamika – the hard-working and very engaged student • Ms. Turner favors relational aspects of teaching math • Deficit oriented language	motivated to complete work on time) • Math is a bunch of rules • A math person is extraordinary, a great thinker • A math person is good with numbers • A math person knows the basics • What does it mean to learn math? • College level math is a hassle • Math doesn't allow room for creativity	to prove stereotypes wrong • Racial socialization • Strong positive identification with being Black • Being Black is a social responsibility • Math identity • Sense of belonging • Membership Vs. Identity • Membership to math community is a personal choice • Membership is unrelated to students' perceived social responsibility	• Sense of belonging • Not interested or capable of seeing themselves as members • Membership not part of their social responsibility (4) Racial socialization (5) Racial hierarchy of math ability

All the Codes that Emerged	Discarded Codes	Codes Used in Presentation and Discussion of Data

• Teacher preparation
• Students' engagement level
• Oxford's culture vs. Classroom culture
• Ms. Turner's beliefs about students' ability
• Ms. Turner's views of students' backgrounds
• Ms. Turner's beliefs about teaching math
• Cecil B. "Moore" student teachers' experiences as a deterrent
• Deficit oriented language
• Students' culture as hindrance
• Students' community as culturally deprived
• Overall math experience
• Positive experiences
• High school math
• Elementary/Middle-school math
• Negative experiences
• Avoidance
• Attitude achievement paradox
• A math person is extraordinary
• A math person is good with numbers
• A math person knows the basics
• What does it mean to learn math?
• Overall math confidence
• Students' perception of a math person
	• Teacher preparation
	• Students' engagement level
	• Deficit oriented language
	• High school math
	• Elementary/ Middle-school math
	• Negative experiences
	• Avoidance
	• Students' community as culturally deprived
	• What does it mean to learn math?
	• Primacy given to relational aspects of teaching
	• Racial socialization
		(1) Math experiences
		   • Mostly positive
		   • Variability in students' interpretation of success in math
		   • Experiences used to delegitimize performance in honor's pre-calculus
		(2) A math person
		   • Predisposed to succeed in math
		   • Knows the rules
		   • Good with money
		   • A great thinker
		(3) Math confidence
		   • Discrepancy in confidence level scores
		   • Sense of belonging
		   • Not interested or capable of seeing themselves as members
		   • Membership not part of their social responsibility
		   • Students feel compelled to disidentify to ensure successful academic and economic future

(*Continued*)

All the Codes that Emerged	Discarded Codes	Codes Used in Presentation and Discussion of Data
• Stereotype threat • Racial identity; racial socialization • Math identity • Sense of belonging • What does it mean to be Black? • Primacy given to relational aspects of teaching		

APPENDIX H: METHODS AND ANALYSIS

Overview of Study

This study used ethnographic methods to collect and analyze data on the mathematics identity construction of 11 students attending Oxford high school, a comprehensive secondary public school located in northeast Philadelphia. Participants were all seniors enrolled in Ms. Turner's honor's pre-calculus; they were in their fourth and final year of secondary school. This study was part of a larger college pipeline and academic enrichment program sponsored by the firm Ernst & Young in partnership with a local state university – the university in question is referred to Cecil B. Moore University throughout this study. Pseudonyms were created and used for every student and teachers mentioned here.

College Pipeline Program

Students recruited into the program were required to take, in the same academic year, one honor's math and one honor's English class. Curricula were designed by a team of Cecil B. University's faculty members, doctoral students, and Oxford teachers.

The program's goal was to ease students' transition from secondary school to higher education. Students were selected based on teacher recommendations, grade point average, attendance and "good" behavior. Everyone enrolled in the college pipeline program received additional support from Ernst & Young staff like mentoring, tutoring, and assistance with college essays. This study's participants had two or more teachers in their honor's pre-calculus and English classes most days of the week. They received a richer, more rigorous, and better supported academic experience relative to other seniors at Oxford high school.

Participant-Observer

I spent 10 months witnessing and experiencing some of the benefits and frustrations inherent to teaching and learning mathematics. I also actively participated in many (side) conversations on topics ranging from sports (e.g., is Lebron James better than Stephen Curry?), the difference between "flirting and cheating," or what a Black teenager from northeast Philadelphia should expect from their first semester at a predominantly white institution. Assuming the role of the dispassionate observer, being the proverbial "fly on a wall," was never a practical or ethical option. I was a researcher who collected copious notes on participants' history with mathematics education and their relationship to the discipline while, also regularly, engaging individual students or small groups in discussions about their lifeworld and future.

Data Analysis

Data collected for this study were a combination of observational (field) notes, informal and semi-structured interviews, a Likert scale survey of students' self reported math confidence (Appendix A), students' attendance, their grade point averages before and in honor's pre-calculus, instructional materials, and other documents related to the college pipeline project.

Preliminary stage – The preliminary stage of data analysis began early. Daily observational (field) notes were transferred from notepads to *Word docx* files at the end of each day. The transfer process entailed a review and fleshing out of field notes. *Word docx*'s "New Comment" and "Track Changes" were used to underline chunks of text that needed to be investigated further. This was an attempt, early on in the study, to identify and track recurring patterns.

Because of the amount of data collected, the use of "analytical memos" was integrated early in the data analysis process. *Memos*, reflective and summative essays inspired by the annotated sections of observational notes and interview transcripts, provided a systematic and analytical way to keep track of both my thoughts and themes. For instance, at the beginning of this study, my first memos were mostly a mixture of complaints for not collecting enough meaningful data and anxiety about my participant-observer role. Toward the end of the study, I used memos as a way to figure out potential relationships between recurring patterns and to allow room for the emergence of new ones.

Semi-structured Interviews

Participants were interviewed twice. The first round took place in the first couple of months of 2016 and the other round began in May of that same year. Interviews were semi-structured. They involved a list of questions; however, interview sessions were guided by each participant's response, as far as length, number of follow-up questions, and how conversational or scripted a session was. The first round of semi-structured interviews focused on establishing each participant's *math autobiography* (Appendix B). The second round of semi-structured interviews centered around each student's *math identity* construction (Appendix C) – the way they defined and related to what it means to be a "math person." Interviews were carefully scheduled so that students did not miss the introduction to a new mathematical concept or an in class assessment. Ms. Turner's office, a small space down the hall from the classroom, was used for the interviews.

Ms. Turner – Ms. Turner, the lead teacher of the honor's pre-calculus class, was also interviewed for this study. By the start of this study, she had been working as a teacher in Philadelphia for more than four decades. Her extensive experience teaching mathematics in underresourced, racially and socioeconomically segregated public schools presented an opportunity to examine the interplay between deficit-laden perception of urban public schools, their students, and existing race-based beliefs that pervade mathematics education.

Data analysis – The combination of 10 months of observations and 22 semi-structured interviews produced about 230 single-spaced pages of transcribed interviews, more than 500 single-spaced pages of field notes, and nine analytical memos. The web application software *Dedoose* was used to help with the triangulation process of the multiple types of data collected. The "Analyze" feature of *Dedoose* was used to identify recurring themes or *codes* that appeared with greater frequency throughout the data. For instance, the *parent code* "Math Experiences" and its *child codes* were applied 85 times; some of those codes like "Positive Experiences," "What it means to learn math," and "Attitude Achievement Paradox" were applied to a significant number of excerpts across interview transcripts, observational notes, and memos.

Memos and a multilevel triangulation of the many types of data collected for this study helped to formulate and shape this study's findings (see Appendix G). The excerpts, coded passages extracted from field notes and students' interview transcripts, were reviewed and analyzed with the objective of piecing together a narrative specific to each parent code. I was also careful to include patterns that either opposed or suggested something different from a recurring theme. For instance, most participants felt positively about their K to 12 experiences in mathematics classrooms. Stephanie and Tamika described their overall experience with math education as a "struggle." Those two seniors had considerable success in mathematics and were among the high performers in the honor's pre-calculus class. Disconfirming evidence or instances like the aforementioned forced me to rethink and revaluate mainstream beliefs about classroom success and its presumed impact on academic identity; it also called for greater attention to students' perception of mathematics education.

INDEX

Printed in the United States
by Baker & Taylor Publisher Services